TIG'S BOYS

Other books by David Hilliam published by The History Press

Kings, Queens, Bones and Bastards
Monarchs, Murders & Mistresses
Crown, Orb & Sceptre
A Salisbury Miscellany
Winchester Curiosities
Why Do Shepherds Need a Bush?
The Little Book of Dorset

TIG'S BOYS

Letters to Sir, from the Trenches

EDITED BY DAVID HILLIAM

First published 2011 by Spellmount,
an imprint of The History Press
The Mill, Brimscombe Port
Stroud, Gloucestershire, GL5 2QG
www.thehistorypress.co.uk

British Library Cataloguing in Publication Data.
A catalogue record for this book is available from the British Library.

ISBN 978 0 7524 6331 5

Typesetting and origination by The History Press
Printed in the EU for The History Press.

CONTENTS

ACKNOWLEDGEMENTS

My thanks are warmly given to the present headmaster of Bournemouth School, Dr Dorian Lewis, for allowing me access to the school archives. I am also greatly indebted to a former pupil of the school, Roger Coleman, MBE, whose own meticulous research into the War Memorials of Bournemouth School enabled me to add information concerning the burial places of every one of Tig's Boys – or in many cases to add information about the exact places where their names are recorded.

The pictures of Dr Fenwick, the school itself and the various groups of academically gifted boys are taken from the school's centenary publication, *Bournemouth School 1901–2000*. I am most grateful to Stuart Wheeler, Assistant Librarian of Bovington Tank Museum, for his help in providing me with the picture of the 'Little Willie' tank (probably the only example of its kind to survive). Equally, I am indebted to Pauline Allwright and Tom Eaton of the Imperial War Museum for their help in finding images for me from their vast picture archive. I am particularly grateful to Mark Warby, in helping me to secure permission from Barbara Bruce Littlejohn (daughter of Bruce Bairnsfather) to use three of Bruce Bairnsfather's famous cartoons.

And finally, my loving thanks go to Jim and Denise Watt for their kindness in sending me the image of the Military Cross, won in Mesopotamia by Denise's grandfather, and which they now hold in safe keeping in Brisbane, Australia.

INTRODUCTION

*B*ournemouth's grammar school for boys was founded in January 1901. No one knew it at the time, but those boys who became pupils there during its first decade were destined to be of fighting age in the world war of 1914–18, arguably the bloodiest war in history.

The War Memorial in the school's entrance hall lists the names of ninety-eight of those young men who were killed in that war. Tragically, this averages about one death every fortnight over the full length of that terrible time.

However, it was not all unrelieved blood and slaughter. Life was hard, but often full of interest and surprise. Those old boys of Bournemouth School constantly wrote back to 'Tig' – their much-respected headmaster – to tell him of their wartime adventures.

Collectively, these letters provide a wide spectrum of the 'Great War.' We read of young men enjoying trying to catch rats in the trenches, winning bets on how long it could take to rescue a tank from no man's land, playing 'footer' amid the gunfire, and singing 'ragtime' in a rickety new-fangled aeroplane while 'rocking the machine in time to it'.

This book is a mosaic of such wartime experiences.

It has been compiled not only to honour the memory of those who lost their lives, but also to show present generations how one typical group of ex-schoolboys coped with circumstances over which they had no control.

They shall grow not old, as we that are left grow old;
Age shall not wither them, nor the years condemn.

A NOTE ON THE TEXT

Mostly, this book is a collection of extracts from the magazine of Bournemouth School, taken either from the letters sent to the headmaster, Dr Fenwick, from ex-pupils who were serving at the Western Front or elsewhere in the world, or else items written by Dr Fenwick himself, such as the obituaries of those who were killed.

The wording of the text is exactly as published in that school magazine. The only editorial changes made are in breaking up some of the very lengthy paragraphs into shorter units, and omitting some personal and extraneous material.

Occasionally, a very long letter has been broken up, so that it appears as two, or even three separate items.

After nearly a century, it has not been thought feasible to contact possible descendants or relations. It is hoped, however, that any descendants who read this book will not be offended, and that they will take pride, as does the school, in the heroism of all those who took part in that terrible 'Great War'.

The First World War, 1914-1918

A BRIEF TIMELINE

1914

4 August .... Britain declares war on Germany
23 August .... Battle of Mons
6–10 September .... Battle of the Marne
19 October–22 November .... First Battle of Ypres

1915

10–13 March .... Battle of Neuve Chapelle
22 April–25 May .... Second Battle of Ypres
22 April .... First use of gas on the Western
Front
25 April–20 December .... Gallipoli expedition
7 May .... Sinking of the *Lusitania*
31 May .... First Zeppelin raid on London
9 October .... British and French troops land at
Salonika, Greece
13 October .... Battle of Loos
13 December .... British and French troops occupy
Salonika

1916

8 January .... Gallipoli evacuation completed
21 February–16 December .... Battle of Verdun

29 April .... British troops surrender at Kut
31 May–1 June .... Battle of Jutland
1 July–18 November .... First Battle of the Somme
15 July–3 September .... Battle of Delville Wood
3 September–23 September .... Battle of Pozières
10 September–19 November .... Allied offensive at Salonika
15 September .... First use of tanks on Western Front

1917

9–14 April .... Battle of Arras
9–14 April .... Battle of Vimy Ridge
7–14 June .... Battle of Messines
31 July–10 November .... Third Battle of Ypres
(Passchendaele)
6 November .... British capture Passchendaele
Ridge
20 November–3 December .... Battle of Cambrai (the first battle
where a large number of tanks are
used – 378)
9 December .... British capture Jerusalem from the
Turks

1918

21 March–4 April .... Second Battle of the Somme
9–29 April .... Battle of the Lys
20–31 July .... Battle of the Marne
5–18 August .... Start of the 'Hundred Days' with
the advance in Flanders
8 August .... British attack at Amiens
(Ludendorff described this as 'the
Black Day' for the German army)
24 August–3 September .... Third Battle of the Somme
18 September–9 October .... Battle of the Hindenburg Line
17 October .... Occupation of Lille
11 November .... Armistice with Germany

TIG AND HIS SCHOOL

Schoolboys have always taken a mischievous delight in finding odd nicknames for their teachers, springing not only from their ingrained impudence, but also – and very frequently – from a special kind of loving respect.

'Tig' was the nickname of Dr Edward Fenwick, first headmaster of Bournemouth's grammar school for boys, from its foundation in 1901 until his retirement in 1932. It was, in fact, short for 'Tiger' – and presumably it reflected Fenwick's unbounded energy and ferocious discipline.

Sadly no one is alive now to give a personal account of this remarkable schoolmaster, but his supreme knack of commanding loyalty and getting the best out of his boys is evident throughout the pages of the school magazine, which he wrote and edited during his long headmastership.

Bournemouth itself had grown up within a generation. Only fifty years before, in 1851, the population had been just 695, but the following decades had seen such swift development that the population had grown to 16,859 by 1881 and to 60,000 by 1901. Thomas Hardy described the land on which Bournemouth was developing in his *Tess of the d'Urbervilles*, published in 1891 – a mere ten years before – remarking that 'not a sod had been turned there since the days of the Caesars'.

By 1901 it was patently obvious that this new town should be provided with good schools. A grammar school was an urgent necessity and accordingly a 'Dr Edward Fenwick, MA, LLD, BSc, Cambridge 10th Senior Optime in Mathematical Tripos, 1890, (late of Wellingborough

Grammar School)' had the good fortune to become its first headmaster. He was to be given a salary of no less than £100 a year plus a capitation fee of £3 per pupil.

THE FIRST DAY

At nine o'clock on Tuesday, 22 January 1901, fifty-four boys assembled in the hall of their brand new school. They must have cringed under the eagle eyes of their fierce, newly-appointed headmaster, Dr Edward Fenwick, and his two full-time and two part-time members of staff.

For just that one day in the life of the school, Queen Victoria was still the reigning monarch. For sixty-three years she had ruled her world-wide empire, latterly from Osborne House on the Isle of Wight, 25 miles away. But this was to be the last day of her reign, and shortly after those fifty-four boys arrived home that afternoon, she died.

Thus it was that when the pupils arrived in school the next morning, the Edwardian Age had begun; a new king, a new school, and a new, exciting century, full of hope and promise. The future beckoned.

THE PRE-1914 YEARS

Tig must have been in his early thirties when he took up his headmastership, and how he relished it.

For most boys it was a day school, serving the Bournemouth area, but Fenwick and his young wife, helped by a 'duly qualified lady matron', looked after a handful of boarders, so for some of his pupils, Tig was very much a father figure. Shortly after taking up his appointment, his wife had twin boys, so the family atmosphere in this small school community must have been apparent.

From fifty-four boys, the school grew rapidly, together with more staff and of course all the familiar activities associated with a busy group of teenagers: football, cricket, OTC (Officers' Training Corps), theatricals,

Gilbert and Sullivan operas, and so on. When an appeal was made for money towards the expenses of Captain Scott's forthcoming expedition to the South Pole, enough money was eagerly subscribed to purchase a sleigh dog.

The school magazine reported that:

> We were kindly allowed to say what name the redoubtable animal should bear on its historic journey. The result was that our representative is to rejoice in the name of 'Tiger'... May he be of a milder nature than his name indicates, and we hope he will return safely after the expedition has successfully attained its object.

Captain Scott himself sent thanks to the boys, though he could hardly have been aware, as the boys were, that Tiger's name had a semi-secret special significance!

The outstanding feature of the school, however, as Tig drove it forward, was its excellent academic results. They were truly phenomenal. Right from the start, Dr Fenwick entered boys for the Cambridge Local Examinations, the equivalent of today's GCSEs and A Levels. In those days there were far fewer candidates, nationally, and although it may seem astonishing to think of it now, Cambridge actually published an order of merit of candidates in each subject.

A memorable photo taken in those years before the First World War shows Tig and three of his pupils: one had been placed first of all 2,419 candidates in the Cambridge Senior Examinations in 1912; another had been placed first out of 2,777 candidates in 1913 and again first out of 2,846 in 1914; and the third had come first out of 3,196 candidates.

These results were no fluke. Boy after boy gained near firsts. In 1917, Fenwick proudly listed nine areas of academic distinction in which the school stood first in England. Another early photo shows fourteen youngsters who had gained various honours in a wide range of subjects. For many years the school achieved the best results of any on the South Coast, and was second best of all the 300 schools entered for the examination – ironically, second only to Wellingborough, Fenwick's previous school.

This, then, was the generation of boys who were called upon to fight in the Great War. Broadly speaking, all pupils who entered Bournemouth School in the first ten years of its existence were eligible to fight. Tragically, they were destined to be subjected to the unimaginable and unprecedented demands made of them by the politicians of their day and the hapless generals.

THE COMING OF WAR
Dr Fenwick's reaction to the situation: a contemporary view

The school magazine of July 1914 has a poignant innocence. It was wholly concerned with school affairs, with no national events casting their shadows. However, it was to be the last of its kind. War was declared the following month, on 4 August, and nothing was to be the same again.

The declaration had come when all the boys were on holiday, so when they reassembled for the Autumn Term, every one of them must have been keenly aware of the dramatic events beginning to take place in France and elsewhere in the world. The autumn magazine of December 1914 spells it out, and Dr Fenwick wrote a solemn account of the situation. Already one master and two old boys had been killed.

The following article by Dr Fenwick in that December magazine is given below – only very slightly abridged. It is quoted at length because it gives a clear indication of the mood of the times. Now, a century later, it can be read as history.

'...A glow of legitimate pride...'

With startling suddenness the greatest war of all time has broken in upon the peace of the world, and at our very doors rages the conflict on the issues of which depend not only the Empire's safety but the very existence, perhaps, of our country as a separate nation.

A careful survey of the official documents issued by the Allies and relating to the events which led up to the war, leads to the conviction that, with the Germans and with them alone, rests the blame for this appalling catastrophe.

Confident in the power of the mighty war-machine which in the last thirty years they had created, they seemed to have resolved to stake all on a war against the powers standing between them and the world domination at which the Prussian military party aimed. True to their reputation, the Balkan States provided the spark which kindled the conflagration, for it was a quarrel between Austria and Servia [sic] that brought about the rupture between Russia and Germany, when France, too, as the ally of Russia, became a party to the war. Though England managed to stand aloof for a short time longer, she was ultimately compelled to take up arms against Germany, when the latter, by invading Belgium, deliberately and for her own ends, broke the treaty guaranteeing the integrity of that country. Alongside the recognition that this war is being waged not against the Germans as a people, grows thee firm conviction that there can be no end to the conflict until the Prussian military despotism has been so completely crushed as to be incapable of further inroads on the world's peace.

To this end it behoves every Briton worthy of the name to be up and doing his utmost, whether it be in the active service of the battlefield or in the more prosaic discharge of the duties which each day brings.

To the call for men our Colonies have responded nobly. The United Kingdom has already enrolled more than a million volunteers, and will find as many more as may be needed. We may well feel proud in these days of stress to be the countrymen of our soldiers now earning for themselves undying fame in France and Belgium, and we may, too, feel a glow of legitimate pride that we are members of a School whose Old Boys have needed no pressing to flock to the colours.

When we consider that the School was opened less than 14 years ago, that not more than twenty of our Old Boys have reached the age of 27, and that the average age is about 21, we can point with much satisfaction to the fact that we know of no fewer than 170 who have come forward to help their country in its time of need by joining some unit of HM Forces.

We are proud of every Old Boy who [has enlisted] and to all we offer our heartiest congratulations and good wishes.

The school magazine, December 1914

In December 1914, no one could have foreseen the terrible carnage that was about to ensue, lasting for more than four years. However, to the very end of the war Dr Fenwick continued to be proud of his boys, encouraging them to enlist and honouring those who were killed in his obituaries of them in successive editions of the school magazine.

It must have been a continual agony of grief as he received message after message telling him of the deaths of his former pupils and staff. In fact, the final number of those killed from Bournemouth School was ninety-eight. It averaged one death every sixteen days – or about two per month throughout the full course of the war.

THE SCHOOL DOES ITS BIT TO HELP WIN THE WAR

While those hundreds of Old Boys were serving in the trenches and on the sea, with a few of them in the air, the boys still at school, encouraged by Tig, were also doing their bit to help win the war.

It was still a horse-drawn, gas-lit world in 1914. A world in which men and boys wore thick, itchy clothes and women wore their skirts and dresses down to the ground. Girls were expected to stay at home with their mothers after leaving their elementary schools, and career opportunities for them were almost non-existent. Bournemouth had not yet thought it worthwhile to provide a grammar school for girls.

Cars were just beginning to trundle over roads not yet ready for them. Cinemas, radios and gramophones were all in their early experimental stages. It was certainly a world without television, videos, mobile phones, computers, central heating or convenience foods. It is probably true to say that none of Tig's boys had ever been abroad.

However, patriotism was paramount, and belts had to be tightened. Sacrifices, however small, were important. Accordingly, 'an appeal was made to the boys to make weekly contributions from their own pocket money to supply our fighting forces with comforts in the way of clothing. The response was most satisfactory, and we were able to send a very useful parcel each week.'

It was recorded that the total sum collected during the first term was twelve pounds, one shilling and ninepence. This may seem a trivial amount today, but it was possibly about the equivalent of Tig's monthly salary.

Woollen garments were also collected, and so were old waste newspapers, the sale of which in the summer of 1916 brought in eleven pounds, four shillings and eight pence for the National War Relief Fund. For this effort, the private secretary to the Prince of Wales – known to later generations as King Edward VIII and subsequently as the Duke of Windsor – wrote a letter to Dr Fenwick to congratulate them on their 'splendid work':

> … by reducing the quantity of paper and paper-making materials imported from abroad… they have helped to retain money in the country and have set free shipping which is badly needed for carrying munitions of war and food. By preventing waste they are helping to provide the sinews of war and so are helping to end the war.

So wrote His Royal Highness, hoping that the boys would continue to collect paper 'with no less enthusiasm in the coming year'.

Perhaps a more immediately practical task undertaken by the boys was their response to an appeal made in March 1916 by the Matron of the local hospital at Boscombe, to supply wooden bedside lockers for the use of wounded soldiers who were in her charge. A quick collection swiftly produced three pounds two shillings, and this went to buy the required timber. By the summer, the boys had produced thirty-four bedside lockers – gratefully accepted by the hospital authorities.

A sacrifice made on his pupils' behalf was Dr Fenwick's decision to abandon the giving of school prizes throughout the duration of the war. The money which would have been spent on these was donated to the war effort, and school successes were rewarded by certificates instead. A considerable amount was raised by this means.

It wasn't all doom and gloom however, for Tig's sense of pride and occasion led to his giving the school a half-day holiday whenever an Old Boy was awarded the Military Cross. Whether this always happened is impossible to say, for there were eighteen such awards, but it must have been a morale booster for the boys, and made them appreciate the courage and honour of their elder brothers and cousins.

At home, the boys would have felt the effects of the war increasingly as food and coal became scarce. Also, Bournemouth was designated as a garrison town for 10,000 troops, and by November 1915 16,000 servicemen were billeted, two or three to a house, in nearly every part of the town. It is most probable that many boys would have had soldiers living temporarily at home with them.

A sad moment came when Lord Kitchener drowned on 5 June 1916, with the sinking of HMS *Hampshire*. It was a moment of national grief and two Old Boys of Bournemouth School also perished in that disaster – Norman Barrow, aged twenty-two, and Ralph Butler, aged twenty (see pages 114 and 118). The Bournemouth Municipal Orchestra played a memorial concert on Bournemouth Pier to an audience of 5,000. Some members of the school must have been in that audience, and their thoughts would inevitably have been with those former fellow pupils, as well as with Lord Kitchener.

The initial outpouring of enthusiasm for the war slowed down as people realised the enormity of it all. 'Home by Christmas!' was the phrase used by those who joined up in 1914 – but by the fourth Christmas there was a dogged determination that however long it might take, the fight must go on.

Dr Fenwick regularly listed the names of all those who were serving – a list which he designated as his 'Roll of Honour'. At Christmas, 1917 – what was mercifully to be the last Christmas of the war – he sent a message to all the hundreds of Old Boys on his Roll of Honour. It captures the spirit of that dark hour:

> In spite of all our hopes the war has extended into a fourth year, and a fourth Christmas finds you still in arms against oppression. At this season, we, your friends at the School (Dr. Fenwick, the Master and Boys) would like to be in your thoughts, as you are in ours, and we send you this card with the assurance of our deep interest in, and close sympathy with you in the time of stress that you are facing with so much courage. We hope that our message may remind you of the happy days you spent here, and that their memory may help you to 'carry on,' patiently and without complaint, until the achievement of that honourable peace for which you are so nobly striving.
>
> *Xmas, 1917*

Dr Fenwick added, in the school magazine of the following March, that 'if one may judge by the number and nature of the replies received, our wishes were very widely and warmly appreciated.'

The following chapters turn to the recipients of that sombre Christmas message. Arguably, their combined experiences provide a microcosm of the conflict that was to be called, without exaggeration, the Great War.

One

LIFE IN THE TRENCHES

War means fighting. However, it also means long periods of discomfort, boredom, dirt, hunger and exhaustion. Those who endured life in the trenches on the Western Front probably remembered the squalor even more than the terror. Nevertheless, these conditions produced camaraderie among those forced to spend weeks and months together.

Arthur Wolfe describes 'our baptism of fire'

You may be interested in reading a short account of how we underwent our baptism of fire.

It was on or about the 20th of last month [January 1915] that we first went into action. The day before we went into billets only a few hundred yards behind our own lines. On the way up a German maxim caught us, but fortunately only two men were wounded. This happened about ten or fifteen yards behind me.

We were in action altogether that time for four days. The trenches when we went in were muddy but not at all bad, but during the time we occupied them we had rain, snow, hail, or sleet all the time, so that it was not very comfortable or pleasant. During the night a pretty heavy fire was maintained, but at day very little was necessary.

We marched to a village about three miles away and after a rub down, a good strong dose of rum, plenty of food and twelve hours' sleep we felt very much better. We have been in action since and feel quite old soldiers now.

At present we are resting, but expect to return to the trenches in about a week's time.

The school magazine, March 1915

Arthur Wolfe describes trench life, '...we fare pretty well'

Our losses to date number four or five killed, and about twenty-four wounded.

I believe in my last letter I related my experiences of one period in the trenches – when we stood in eighteen inches of mud for sixteen hours, suffered intensely from the cold, and came out wet through and through.

The conditions were altogether different in the period just completed. I was in the trenches for eleven hours at night. It was a beautiful moonlight night, consequently we had to use extreme care getting in and out in case we should be seen. The trench was perfectly dry, and the only thing that worried us was the cold.

This part of the line is rather advanced, and, therefore, no advantage would be gained by either side advancing at present. Things were very quiet indeed. You will understand how quiet it was when I tell you that we felt more real security in the trenches than in the billets which we occupied a few hundred yards in the rear of our position. Twice whilst there we made preparations to retire to bomb-proof dug-outs. German shells were flying all round us – the other buildings very close to us were hit, but fortunately we escaped.

We are at present enjoying a few days' rest, but expect to be sent back to the firing-line at any time.

Work in the front line of the trenches is not the hardest part of the campaign. At times we have occupied reserve trenches, where there is nothing to do but keep a good look-out. Cold monotonous work, this!

Then we have a lot of long marching to do from one point of the line to another, which carrying a heavy pack on your back, tires one out more than anything else.

For billets we generally are housed in barns, with or without roofs, but taking everything into account, we fare pretty well in this respect.

The school magazine, March 1915

Arthur Wolfe wrote this on 4 March 1915. He was killed one week later.

2nd *Lieutenant Henry Budden* has a 'marvellous escape'

I am now second in command of a battery of trench Howitzers attached to the 8th Division, and very nice little toys they are too. We have four guns, which throw quite a decent-sized shell filled with shrapnel, and they have an explosion like a 6-inch Howitzer.

It is the German machine guns that do the damage. They are awfully clever with them, as we found the last time this Battalion attacked. I shall not forget it for a long time. They also seemed to find a lot of big gun ammunition, but their shells, and especially their shrapnel, are not a patch on ours, but nevertheless one of them blew up 20 of my platoon, and my escape was marvellous. I was right in the middle of a group of 25 men, 14 of whom were killed and seven wounded, but I was only knocked down by a sod of earth and was not one whit the worse for my fall.

I am now some two miles behind the firing line at a place the Huns have knocked to pieces, but still the civilians live on here in spite of an almost daily shelling.

The school magazine, July 1915

Henry Budden wrote this on 4 June 1915. He was killed four months later.

2nd Lieutenant Arnold Whitting
arrives at the Front

On the way I could see where the firing line was, owing to the many star-lights that were sent into the sky. These present quite a pretty sight and look rather like a firework display. From where I was it appeared as though I was completely surrounded, for these star-lights could be seen in every direction. It is really because, in this part, we are on a salient which makes a full semi-circle.

The next day I was told to go up into the trenches with the transport which takes up the rations. It was pouring with rain, and we had a walk of seven miles. The Belgian roads were in an awful state and we were continually treading in shell-holes.

By the time I arrived at the Battalion Headquarters I was absolutely drenched through and through. My Company was in the trenches at the time, so I had to go straight in as I was, and there I remained for two more days.

The school magazine, December 1915

Arnold Whitting enjoys seeing an irate
sergeant-major getting stuck in the mud

The trenches were the last word in mud. Several times I was stuck and had to be pulled out, and, to a spectator, it would present rather a comical sight no doubt. When a party of men are detailed for a fatigue, they often have to stop while someone is pulled out. I remember seeing one poor chap having to leave his gum-boots stuck in the mud and push along in his socks!

I shall never forget one little incident. I was in the fire-trench, and just behind me were some men working at a dug-out. Presently a very irate sergeant-major came stumping along to tell them they were not doing it to his liking.

Suddenly he stuck in the mud and couldn't move. There he was, purple in the face, and condemning everyone to most unpleasant places! I had to turn away: it was really too funny for words. To add to his discomfort one of his boots refused to move, and he eventually stumbled away with one boot on and one boot off.

Although some of the men can hardly feel their feet owing to the wet and cold, they still remain cheerful. I think that was what impressed me most. Whatever were the conditions they always made the best of things.

The school magazine, December 1915

2nd Lieutenant Arnold Whitting tells of fatigue parties and the German snipers

I think while I was out here I experienced some of the worst weather they have had as all. In several places the trenches were falling in, which, naturally entailed a great deal more work.

There are fatigue parties detailed night and day, and they usually have to work four hours at a stretch. There has been no real fighting near our quarter for some time, although artillery has been pretty active.

Unfortunately German snipers are very smart, and have secured many victims who shewed themselves only for a moment.

The school magazine, December 1915

Later in the war, Arnold Whitting was awarded the Military Cross.

G.A. Turner, briefly away from the trenches, tries to buy some toothpaste in French

I wanted to buy some tooth-paste, and I had to gaze for many minutes into the window of a chemist's shop before I completed this master-piece: 'Je désire quelque chose à laver mes dents.'

Before I was word perfect a girl pounced on me. She was so animated that I was terrified and nearly fled. However, I bubbled out my little phrase, and subsequently many more little phrases.

**** was quite jealous. I'm quite braced with the pronunciation of French à la Bournemouth School. ****'s pronunciation is appalling: he was at **** School. However, he doesn't come near to ****. He jumped into a cab at Havre and shouted with much gusto to the cabby chap: 'A la guerre, à la guerre, vitement!' meaning, of course, 'à la gare.'

The school magazine, December 1915

2nd Lieutenant G.A. Turner has a trench named after him

2nd lieutenant G.A. Turner, transferred from 3rd Dorsets to the Royal Flying Corps, whilst with the former contingent had a great deal of work to do in the trenches. By command of Brigade Headquarters a trench was name after him, 'Trench Turner,' in recognition of recon-noitring work done by him when he crept up to within ten yards of the German lines and obtained some valuable information.

Dr Fenwick, writing in the the school magazine, December 1915

2nd Lieutenant Edwin Hill goes flat on the ground when 'star shells' appear in the sky

I have been up into the front line trenches several times, and the day before yesterday I saw (through a periscope) the rifle of a German sniper who had established himself only 15 yards away from our trenches. He and one of our own snipers were exchanging shots all the time I was there.

It is rather trying work digging trenches close to the firing line at night. The Germans send up very brilliant 'star shells' at frequent intervals during the night. The only thing for us to do is to go flat on the ground until they die out.

The officer who was sharing my billet with me was unfortunately hit, along with three of his men, by a rifle grenade yesterday morning, so am now by myself.

The school magazine, December 1915

Lance Corporal A.H. Rogers learns a useful tip about how to fix detonators in bombs

By going on a special bombing course I get let off fatigues for a fortnight. The lectures are really interesting and the sergeant adds to the interest by telling us chatty little anecdotes of 'Sergeant So-and-so, who had his hands blown off when fixing a detonator, and Lieut. So-and-so, who was blown to pieces while taking charge of a bombing practice,' etc. All this adds to the interest.

I have done quite a lot of odd jobs... such as fixing detonators in bombs. This is a somewhat ticklish job, and the instructor always tells you to hold the detonator between thumb and forefinger as it is better to have those two blown off than the whole of your hand.

P.S. I am a fully paid Lance Corporal now, getting 3d a day more than as a private and doing about six times as much work!!

The school magazine, December 1915

R. Tyson relates how the Germans taunt the English

Whilst in the firing line of these trenches I had about two hours sleep per night, so that all the spare time during the day was used for sleeping.

We get papers a day late, and it is interesting to note what mistakes are made almost daily in news of this district.

Yesterday, when a certain Battalion relieved us, the Germans shouted out 'Come on S*****s' [the name of the regiment]. It is most extraordinary how they learn what is going on here so quickly. They also, in one part of 'No man's land,' had placed a notice (by night) in English: – 'Lemberg is taken and the Russians are retreating, the French are no good, and we can eat you English!'

The school magazine, July 1916

R. Tyson enjoys a few days of well-earned leisure

We are again in billets after a fortnight in the trenches. Much of that time was passed in 'paddling' along trenches which were in most parts 6ins deep in water, other parts being very sticky or very slippery, as it was a clay district – some very famous brickfields. The rain was very heavy at times – now the heat is quite oppressive.

I have a bed to sleep in (mirabile dictu) and the Officers' Mess is a large room about 35ft by 20ft in a big house surrounded by a garden. Behind the Mess there is a conservatory containing unripe grapes. We are quite lucky here.

Yesterday we had some sports, which we finish to-night at 6 p.m. (unless spies have sent word to the Hun artillery about the meeting!)

I ran with 29 men of A Company in the 1,000 yards race. Last night we ran off the first heats of 100 yards, potato race, tug-of-war (also horseback tug-of-war, which was very ludicrous), etc.

At present I am sitting on my bed, frequently dropping the pencil to kill flies, which are as usual innumerable, with a piece of thin leather attached to a stick.

... P.S. Would you like any bits of shells, etc?

The school magazinee, July 1916

W.J. Ray, with 'heavy artillery', finds that 'German aeroplanes are our chief worry'

At present we are at a quiet part of the line and we have not been worried much by 'Fritz' yet. Up to now we seem to have been doing the worrying for we have had one or two little bombardments of our own which he has not answered.

It is easy at night to follow the trenches, which are not very far off. Machine guns are constantly going and all along the line the star shells are sent up. These make rather a fine sight for they light up all the country like day.

Another fine sight that we see nearly every sunny day is the shelling of aeroplanes. The little shrapnel clouds burst without any warning near the aeroplane, which flies very high. After a few seconds the explosion of the shell may be heard, and then other small clouds will appear generally nearer and nearer to the plane. It is not very often, however, that we have to shell German planes, for not many come over, but our own do a good deal of work.

German aeroplanes are our chief worry, for we have to be very careful in disguising our positions to give them no information as to our position. Should they get an idea where we were they would very soon send over something and we would have to move – if there was anything to move.

The school magazine, December 1916

How temporary 2nd Lieutenant H.A. Short gained the Military Cross

H.A. Short was awarded the Military Cross for conspicuous gallantry in action.

As bombing officer during an attack he shewed [sic] the greatest courage in maintaining the bomb supply and directing carrying-parties under heavy artillery and machine gun fire.

He was decorated by the King at the investiture on November 4th [1916], and returned to the front soon afterwards.

Dr Fenwick writing in the school magazine, December 1916

A.H. Rogers is assured that he has lice in his clothes

The men in the regiment are rough diamonds, but very good fellows, and they made us welcome when we arrived.

It was amusing to see them sitting round the fire in the barn which is our billet, killing lice in their clothes. Everyone abounds in lice here, but so far I've not suffered, though I'm assured by the old hands that I must have them on me by now.

We are expected to clean buttons and badges though all our cleaning tackle was taken away from us when we came out and none of us have anything at all.

The school magazine, March 1917

E.A.A. Chudleigh is put in charge of horses

I am glad the people in England seem to be realising, at last, what a big thing we are engaged in – out here that fact is forced upon one at every turn, and, in the face of everything, there is scarcely a despondent face out here.

Louse-killing, as described by Mr A.H. Rogers, a master at Bournemouth School (1911–46), was a common sight. Clothes of all soldiers were infested with these pale fawn creatures, and it became a communal leisure activity to sit around killing off one's 'chatts' – the popular name for these lice.

Soldiers would search their uniforms and underwear, especially in the seams, and crack the chatts between the thumb-nails. Another technique was to run the seams over a candle flame. Success in killing them was heard by a loud crackling noise. If you squashed them, they squirted blood – your own!

Special delousing stations were established, but it was easier to deal with the little pests yourself, as and when you had the time to do it.

Apparently, the chatts liked the warmth of the men's clothes. One old soldier made the macabre observation that when a man was killed, the creatures soon left the corpse to seek a better home.

I came across a bunch of men a day or two ago laying bets on which plot of ground the next shell would pitch – it never seemed to occur to them that it might be the one they were standing on.

I am transport officer to this Battalion now; it always strikes me as being rather funny my having been trained as a motor engineer and always being a great advocate of motor traction, and here I am in charge of the horseflesh end of the Battalion.

The school magazine, March 1917

Lieutenant H.G. Head repairs his tank at night

On one occasion when he was in action, and his tank in 'No Man's Land' it was struck by a German shell, which destroyed the clutch. Unable to move the machine, he and his men were obliged to abandon it and retire to their own trenches.

When night came they returned to the 'Tank' with the tools and spare parts necessary to do the repairs, but they were 'spotted' by a German searchlight and, the neighbourhood having become very 'unhealthy', they were obliged to discontinue their work and again retire.

They by no means gave up hope of retrieving their derelict tank, however, and the next day, under the cover of a friendly fog, they went out again, completed the repairs, and brought back the Tank in triumph.

We understand that, though barely 22 years old, Lieut. Head has been recommended for a 'Captaincy.'

Dr Fenwick, writing in the school magazine, March 1917

Lieutenant H.G. Head is awarded an Military Cross for a 'brilliant exploit' with his 'tank'

'The General Officer Commanding-in-Chief has, under the authority granted by HM the King, awarded the Military Cross to Temp. Lieut. H. G. Head, Heavy Machine Gun Corps, for gallantry in the field.'

It seems that, in one of the 'scraps' on the Western Front, a detachment of our infantry was badly mauled, in an attempt to rush a German trench, by a concealed machine gun. Lieut. Head and another officer, each in command of a 'Tank' were then sent to see what they could do. The other 'Tank' appears to have stuck fast, but Head's went on and 'sat' across the enemy trench, enfilading* it, and, incidentally, knocking out the hidden machine gun.

Lieut. Head was warmly congratulated on his well-deserved decoration by the General commanding his Division, his Lieut. Colonel, and the OC his Battalion.

Dr Fenwick writing in The Bournemouth, *March 1917*

*Enfilading: 'To be in a position to discharge firearms along the whole length of a line.'

HOW THE TANK GOT ITS NAME

It's interesting to notice that Dr Fenwick uses inverted commas for the word 'Tank' and actually gives it a capital letter. It's a measure of how strange and new this war machine was.

When the army tank was first invented by the British in the First World War, it was known, for secrecy, as a 'water-carrier for Mesopotamia'. It was an arbitrary code-name, but the workmen manufacturing it took the name up literally and called it 'that tank thing', in reference to the term 'water-carrier'. The inventor himself, Sir Ernest Swinton, then suggested adopting the word 'tank'.

In the Second World War, Hitler wanted a nice German-based word to replace the English word 'tank'. But the suggested replacement – schutzen-grabenvernichtungsapparat – somehow didn't quite catch on.

E.J.H. Douch goes ratting with petrol

... after dinner, a rat hunt was proposed. Armed with spades and electric torches we went to some old trenches, which we knew were infested with the rodent.

The process is to pour petrol down the holes, to ignite it, and to wait for the unfortunate occupiers to come out into the light of the torches. This, by the way, gives rise to the popular supposition, which is quite erroneous, that petrol, Shell A, is supplied by an indulgent Government to be used in stoves and for ratting expeditions, while what is left over may be used to drive aeroplanes.

The proceedings terminated at 11.30 p.m. with not a single rat to our credit, but many narrow escapes, for it is apt to be dangerous, when half-a-dozen people are close together, attempting to strafe one frightened animal.

The school magazine, April 1917

W.J. Wray is lucky to be billeted in wooden huts with nearby bathing facilities

... we are billeted in small wooden huts and foraging expeditions are frequently made to keep us in firewood. This is a necessity when, as now is the case, there is about three or four inches of snow lying everywhere.

We are near a village which is used for billeting and contains an old dye works, which has been turned into a bathing establishment. This is like the baths illustrated some time ago in one of the weekly papers. Clean underclothes are exchanged for one's dirty linen, and tunics and trousers are fumigated. Meanwhile the luxury of a bath in hot water is indulged in, and after the process is completed you feel like a different person.

The school magazine, April 1917

H.B. Footner arrives 'somewhere in France' 8 chevaux, 40 hommes

We crossed the Channel and were stationed at one of our huge base camps. On our first day there we were given an experience of the gas, passing through it in gas helmets, but the rest of our time there, nearly a month, was occupied with nothing but fatigues.

These varied from timber carrying to road sweeping, and as we were working all the week, except on Sunday afternoon, and were fetched out of our tents at four in the morning, we had an experience that none of us want repeated.

Our journey up here to our base depot lasted 26 hours, and was made in one of those delightful trucks labelled '8 chevaux, 40 hommes!'

The school magazine, July 1917

S.W. Tucker plays 'footer' amid the gun-fire

You would be rather surprised to see the position of our cricket and footer grounds, with the guns continually firing all around us.

Sometimes the old Boche will send over a few when we get nicely settled down to a game, which rather upsets things for a while, but we soon carry on. There is not much that will worry the British Tommy. At any rate, that is my experience of him.

The school magazine, July 1917

Lieutenant E.W. Little looks around some 'decidedly interesting' captured german pill-boxes

The pill-boxes are decidedly interesting, and provide excellent protection from shell fire and bombs. One is never tired by monotony in moving from one pill box to others, for no two are alike.

One I occupied for about three weeks was so small that though it was a very comfortable place in which to sleep, one could not stand up, but had to crawl to get from one side of the room to the other. The ceiling was only about four feet from the ground, so one had to sit upon the floor to carry out the ordinary duties in connection with the battery. This pill-box was situated in a trench and could not be seen from outside, so it must have proved a formidable spot to our troops when they attacked the trench.

Another pill-box I occupied for a few days was much more comfortable, having bunks for sleeping and a roof about six feet which led into

In nearly every case where the churches are ruined the crucifix remains standing, like a monument amidst all this destruction.

S.W. Tucker, July 1917

a long strongly protected room; a door in this led to an inner room, fitted with bunks and cupboards, while a tunnel joined this to a third room. A ladder in this room led to an opening in the roof, which was used by the Hun as an observation post.

I found another very clever observation post quite by accident a few weeks ago. That, too, was German. A tree on a hill had been cut down at about three feet from the ground and the inside hollowed out. A hole had then been cut facing what was then our lines. The observer had his post underground and a periscope was placed so that its object-glass fitted the hole cut for it, giving the observer a perfect view of our lines, with no risk to himself.

I saw yet another OP [observation post], which I should not like to have occupied myself. A ladder, about 50 feet long, fixed to a tree, gave access to the top of the tree, which formed the observation post. Once there, the observer would have to stay till dusk, with no protection from shrapnel or other shell fragments.

The school magazine, December 1917

Four miles advance – 'and such mud!'
(As described by Lieutenant E.W. Little)

We have been very active indeed during the last three months, and so big has been the advance on this front that the Battery has moved forward four miles in that time.

It is impossible to realise at home what that move means! The advance has been over land which is naturally marshy, and into which thousands of shells have been poured, with the result that the ground is covered with craters partially filled with water, and consequently not suitable for the movement of pieces of ordnance.

The roads, too, suffered considerably as a result of artillery activity, so that, when you search for a road marked 'First Class' on the map, you probably recognise it by the stumps of trees which once lined it, while you are standing in six inches of mud – and such mud!

It seems to have been produced to delay progress, for it clings very closely to one's boots, and after a walk through it, all signs of polish from toe to knee of the boot have disappeared, and you carry back several pounds of mud.

The school magazine, December 1917

Lieutenant A.H. Baker wins a bet with his Commanding Officer, by rescuing a tank within a given time

I am in charge of a section of the Tank Salvage Company. Our duty is firstly to lend a helping hand when a 'stunt' is taking place and afterwards to recover if possible the derelict Tanks.

On a recent occasion I was ordered to salve whole a Tank that Fritz had evidently made good target practice on.

Tank fully equipped weighs about 30 tons, i.e. equals the weight of say three of the Corporation steam rollers. Under skilful manipulation it can perform marvellous operations, from climbing over trenches and through shell craters to standing on its head or its tail or climbing over a sister tank, but the chief trouble of the commander is the awfully boggy ground.

We found that the particular Tank referred to had been badly ditched, or in other words had sunk deep into the bog. The first thing to do was to get inside of it and find out if the engine were in likely working order. We found two of the cylinders and the radiator smashed by shell fire, and the gears damaged, but otherwise it appeared to be all right.

Preparations were then made for clearing a passage way – this had to be done by the men with their hands. Once the spade was in the mud one could not lift it up, but had to pull the spadeful off by hand – some game! The next job was to take away the damaged cylinders and renew the gears, also fix up an improvised radiator made from empty oil drums.

After much labour we at last got away, but I found we could steer only a straight course. Owing to the condition of the ground we could not swing right or left, and in front of us was a belt of trees and more marshy ground. However, there was no help for it but to go straight ahead and trust in Providence.

A large tree was the first obstacle, and the Tank was elevated in front and put in motion, so that by sheer weight it brought down the tree, which, falling across part of the boggy ground, gave us a fairly good footing by which to crawl across.

We had not proceeded very far on our way when we came across an artillery officer with about 100 men vainly attempting to drag a big gun drawn by a tractor out of a similar plight. Labour as they might they could not make it budge.

I then asked the officer if I could be of any use, and looking at our battered old 'bus he says, 'No thank you, that thing is no good.'

I then bet him a 'Gold Flake' that if he would let me try I would fetch it out. This he willingly agreed to and we soon had our hauling tackle fastened to his gun, much to the astonishment and gratification of the Tommies, who soon had the pleasure of seeing gun and tractor hauled out bodily by the derelict old 'bus.

Shortly afterwards we came under gas shells, but we were well equipped against gas attack, and we wended our way homewards, and in due course arrived at our destination.

There I had the satisfaction of drawing a sovereign from my CO, who had made me a bet that we would not bring it back within a given time. This I divided among the crew, who well deserved it.

The school magazine, December 1917

F.J.D. Lonnen suffers shell shock and is discharged after twenty months in the firing line

After spending about twenty months in the firing line in France, I am very thankful to write that I have been fortunate enough to arrive home in 'Blighty' again.

'BLIGHTY'

'Blighty', for all those serving abroad, was a magically nostalgic word for 'England' or 'home'. It is thought to be a corruption of the Hindustani word *bilaik*, 'foreign country', and especially England.

It came to signify anything good, used as an adjective, e.g. 'This is real Blighty butter', meaning ideal, excellent, of home-quality. A wounded soldier would be given a 'Blighty Bag' at a Casualty Clearing Station, to hold his personal possessions.

To get a 'Blighty One' was a real hope and dream for those at the front. It meant getting a wound that was not life-threatening, but serious enough to enable a soldier to be sent back home to recover.

It was not at all unknown for a man to inflict a wound on himself, hoping to be regarded as having received a 'Blighty One'. One old soldier, writing after the war, claimed that many men – 'perhaps all men at certain times' – felt ready to lose a leg or an arm in exchange for a permanent return to 'Blighty'.

The Battery to which I belonged was a time-serving one, namely the [sic] Heavy Battery. I joined them in November, 1915. During the 'Great Offensive,' which commenced on July 1st, 1916 (the Battle of the Somme) we were all kept very busy and were firing incessantly both day and night. Several of our fellows were awarded DCMs [Distinguished Conduct Medal], Military Medals, etc.

After the taking of Bapaume, our Battery moved way to another part of the line nearer Bethune, Mazingarb, Lens, and Loos. 'Fritz' tried very hard to break through here, but we pushed him back 'slowly but surely.'

The school magazine, December 1917

Lieutenant A.H. Baker's first night near the fighting line

I well recollect and shall never forget my first night near the fighting line, as for hours I lay on the roof of a cottage and heard the thunder of the heavy guns and witnessed the marvellous illumination of the sky by innumerable rockets, flares and signals of every description. This was war, but on a scale vastly greater than I had ever pictured or contemplated.

I will not attempt to harrow your feelings by telling you of the gruesome sights I have since seen or my first experience under shell fire, but I am proud to bear witness to the indomitable pluck and cheerfulness of officers and men under the most trying circumstances.

The school magazine, December 1917

Why 2nd Lieutenant Maurice Hellier needs to be 'in a recumbent position'

Within the somewhat cramped interior of the 'Mess,' for our quarters always seem to go by the conventional name, however unconventional they may be in reality, three of us are variously employed. One is engaged in an earnest endeavour to re-discover the lower part of his face from beneath a three days' growth of his beard. Judging by an occasional exclamation his efforts are meeting with somewhat painful and unexpected success. The other is playing a desultory game of Patience in a corner, and I am lying in my bunk writing.

The value of performing all possible operations in bed cannot be over-rated as an economy of space. We write letters, eat our meals, and do as many other odd jobs as possible in a recumbent position, simply because by that means we are less likely to become generally unpopular.

When the mere fact of A moving his foot will certainly knock B's cup of tea over, or, if he is lucky enough to avoid that, will be bound to result in his treading on C's shaving brush, and when B stands up, C inevitably falls down as they are both sitting on a home-made bench with one central leg – it will be seen there are occasions when lying down has enormous advantages over any more upright position.

The school magazine, March 1918

Maurice Hellier is confused by trench systems 'which defy description'

The method of construction was evidently on a piecemeal principle, and the resulting confusion of passages and staircases defies description.*

It is well when one takes a walk in this labyrinth not to attempt to get to any particular place, but to adopt the mental attitude of a sightseer who is prepared to go anywhere and see anyone or anything.

Should you be so foolhardy as to attempt the strong-minded course of setting out with a purpose you will probably be still engaged on the job when peace is declared, by which time the matter will have become such an obsession that you will be unable to tear yourself away.

On the other hand, if you firmly reject all thoughts of your particular needs or duties and set forth, you will invariably meet just the man you want round the first corner.

Another playful little habit of the builders was to make all, or nearly all, the dimensions a size too small. In the passages there is seldom room for two to pass and one has always to go about in a stooping attitude to avoid severe collision between one's head and the roof.

Their crowning triumph in this direction, however, is to be found on the staircases; these are so much undersized that whether the new arrival decides to go down in a straightforward manner or to tackle the business backwards, he must inevitably either hit his face against the roof at every step or rub his chin in the mud.

Such is the place which by contrast with winter weather conditions in the front line is a haven of peace and comfort to get back to for a day or so.

In spite of the underground atmosphere created by 400 human beings and the discomfort of six inches of water in the passages in wet weather, the feeling of security and a good night's sleep are worth a lot at such a time, and our thanks are certainly due to those Companies of the REs who made the place, and if we grouse they certainly have the right to say with "Alf," 'If you knows of a better 'ole, go to it!'

The school magazine, March 1918

*The dug-outs (i.e. trenches)... are a whole series of connected saps (see box opposite).

2nd Lieutenant A.C. Howard – 'an inspiring example to all'

A.C. Howard, 2nd Lieutenant, Hants Regiment, has been awarded the Military Cross. The order reads as follows:

'For most conspicuous gallantry, good leading and devotion to duty in the attack on September 26th and 27th [1917]. He led his platoon during the attack with determination and although a heavy mist made direction difficult, he led his men by compass bearing on his objective under very heavy shell and machine gun fire.

In the advance he organised and led small bombing parties, and cleared all the dug-outs in his advance. When the final objective was taken he assisted in organising his Company, and did most valuable work in consolidating the captured positions. His energy, cheerfulness, and contempt for danger were an inspiring example to all.'

The school magazine, April 1918

FRONT, SUPPORT, RESERVE, AND SAPS

It's easy to imagine that the Western Front consisted of just one long, straight line of trenches. However, in fact there were three parallel lines, often consisting of a rambling, confusing jumble of interconnected dug-outs – as Maurice Hellier described them in the previous item opposite. And then these three parallel lines of trenches were linked to one another by 'saps'.

The Front Line, as its name implies, was the one which immediately faced the enemy, and provided the position from which to fight and shoot.

Behind this was the Support Line, sometimes called the Travel Trench; which enabled men to move about in relative safety and bring up supplies of ammunition, food and equipment.

Finally, at the rear, was the Reserve Trench, where there were various stores, officers' dug-outs, kitchens, latrines, etc.

To add to the confusion, the lines were made to zig-zag, so as to prevent enemy intruders shooting along whole lengths of a trench (enfilading).

The main links between the Front Line and the Supports and Reserves were called Communication Trenches. The 'saps' were smaller lines of communication. Trenches were made by digging downwards; saps were made by digging outwards from an existing trench. Almost invariably, it was the infantry who dug both saps and trenches.

The words 'sapper' and 'sap' ultimately derive from the Latin *sappa*, a pick.

The following letter is probably describing the battle of Lys, 9–29 April 1918:

2nd Lieutenant R.A. Curties, with the 'heavies' enjoys 'a certain exhilaration about open warfare'

I had a fairly peaceful time till the 9th April, when things moved quickly for a few days. We came out with a loss of two guns and with but few casualties. All my kit went 'West' with the gun so I was reduced to borrowing even soap and towel for about a week.

There was but little sleep or rest for anyone those first few days, but there is a certain exhilaration about open warfare which made itself felt by all of us. To have seen the guns being brought into action and pulled out again in one position after another would have impressed anyone with the mobility of the 'Heavies.' The MT stood up to the work splendidly and not a single engine went 'dud.'

It was great to be free from the continual worry of 'camouflage' and tracks.

In one position all four guns were in a large field behind a farm, which was made our HQ.

Right in the open, all in a line, with their noses stuck wickedly into the air, they looked fine. Never once did the ammunition fail us, and I have never known the guns to get so hot as they did in those few days.

Things were sorted out afterwards, but for a few days guns were left in the positions to which they had been rushed.

To our rear at the place I mention were eleven 60 pdrs. [pounders]. In a row, their picket lamps at night reminding one of the Brighton front before the war.

The continual pad-ang of their 'double report' did not increase our love for the guns, especially when trying to get to sleep on a cold night without blankets.

We were troubled with our own 'Hows' [Howitzers] too, as No. 1 was directly behind the mess and every time it fired down came the

---

HOWITZER

A 'howitzer' was a short, squat gun which lobbed heavy shells on a very high trajectory, so that they came down almost vertically on their targets. It is in interesting word, derived from the German *Haubitze*, which in turn was derived from the Czech *houfnice* – a sling.

dust, etc., from the roof and there was a rush to cover the butter or the jam.

The school magazine, July 1918

Mr Rogers was a master at Bournemouth School, joining the staff in 1911. He survived the war, returned to his teaching post, and retired in 1946 – after the end of the Second World War. In 2010 some old pupils still remembered him with respect and affection.

A.H. Rogers sees huge woods absolutely blown to atoms

We are in a different sector of the line, though not far away from where we were before, and here our lines are much nearer the Boche, so that in addition to the inevitable 5.9's etc. we also have to put up with 'Minnies'* – very unpleasant they are, too.

I say 'we' advisedly, for I am not in the line, but back with the Brigade, but I visit the forward areas daily and don't waste any time about it either. However, we are tolerably safe – safer than if we were further back, for the Boche shells back-areas regularly now and huts do not offer the best protection against HV Shells and 9 inchers.

The country round here is more devastated than any part of the line. I have seen huge woods absolutely blown to atoms. I often wonder how on earth we ever took these places; it speaks volumes for the efficiency of the gunners that they ever were taken the Boche must have literally been blown out of them. He certainly chose his places well, for the observation that he must have got from them is truly remarkable.

The school magazine, July 1918

*A 'Minnie' was a shortened form of *Minenwerfer* – the German word for mine-thrower, i.e. bomb-thrower. It also referred to the bomb itself, which the Tommies also called a 'football', 'rum jar' or 'Christmas pudding'.

A.H. Rogers and the unprintable remarks made about 'now buy a war bond'

Everybody is frightfully keen on salvage, and you are exhorted never to return from the front line without salving something. It is quite a common thing to see a notice board put up asking you to carry something to the Brigade Salvage Dump and a little further on a board with the following inscription: 'Thank you – now buy a War Bond.'

Tommy resents the latter very much, and his remarks are amusing, if unprintable.

A.H. Rogers, quoted in the school magazine, July 1918

Mr E.W. Little sees a village crucifix

... one sees heaps of barbed wire scattered over the country, but that is a necessary adjunct to any defensive system.

Near the line one also sees heaps of bricks and portions of walls, where once stood happy villages, but the wave of battle has swept over them, and the ruins mark its path.

Yet the ruin is not complete, for in each of these villages, often untouched, stands a huge crucifix. One, within a few hundred yards of our trenches, was hit by a 'dud' shell, which firmly embedded itself in the wood of the cross without overthrowing it.

The school magazine, July 1918

It's astonishing how cheerful the Tommies keep...

... one notices it in censoring letters. Very rarely does one come across any complaints, though they 'grouse' all day long. I often think one could not exist without 'grousing.' Everybody does it and everybody is convinced that he is the most hardly used person on earth.

I heard a New Zealander holding forth on the new Boche long

range gun that has been firing on Paris. Quoth he: 'If the **** Boche use this **** gun on this front, our **** Brigade HQ will establish itself in a **** pillbox in New Zealand.'

Mr A.H. Rogers (a master) quoted in the school magazine, July 1918

2nd Lieutenant A.H. Baker MC and Bar. How A.H. Baker gained his second Military Cross

The following is the War Office report: 'Nov. 7th [1918], Bar to Military Cross, T/2nd-Lieut. A. H. Baker, MC. Tank Corps, for conspicuous gallantry and devotion to duty.'

He worked with unremitting energy for three days and nights, with little sleep, at the arduous work of salving damaged Tanks.

He was under heavy shell fire practically the whole time, and he and his detachment had to work in gas masks as the locality was saturated with gas. He showed a fine example of determination and disregard of danger.

The school magazine, December 1918

2nd Lieutenant J.D. Sinclair and the 'marvellous effect' of 'ten minutes intense'

I am greatly interested in my new hobby of strafing the Boche; it is very amusing sometimes. A Boche battery may be shelling Brigade Headquarters or some other battery. An urgent message comes down on the phone, 'ten minutes intense,' and the co-ordinates of the Boche battery.

We sit in a cellar and work out a few angles, one sub goes down to the guns, and we 'ten minutes intense.' The effect is marvellous. Although we cannot see his battery, and have no idea what size the guns composing it are, it is silenced for a time.

Just as a congratulatory message comes down from the Brigade, the Boche starts again, and we have to give him a little more. It is a wonderful game.

We are in a house, the fourth from the end of the road. This is lucky because the end house stops everything which the Boche sends over in our direction. Sometimes we have finished our 'soup' and are waiting for our 'fish', watching the candle (stuck in a whisky bottle) start and flicker, as a gun near by goes off. Suddenly there is a whistle, gradually getting louder, and then a crash. 'The end house,' we all murmur, and some wag adds, 'Long may it live.'

As the Boche has started again I expect we shall get some 'intense' in a minute, so I will bring my letter to a close.

The school magazine, December 1918

Captain J.L. Furness gets a 'cushy' wound – 'Am I not lucky?'

A few nights ago three of us (officers) and nearly 100 men carried out a raid on the Boches' trenches at 1.20 in the morning. The whole show was a great success, and we took a number of prisoners and a machine-gun, besides inflicting heavy casualties while in his lines.

The three officers were wounded together with about 40 of our boys, but everything that was demanded of us was carried out and our Brigadier General and Colonel were delighted with the whole show.

... I am lying in bed with a nice 'cushy' wound. I have stopped a piece of shell this time in my right calf. A small operation soon extricated this nuisance, and I am now as comfortable as ever. In a few days' time I hope to be on my way to England.

Am I not lucky?

The school magazine, December 1918

A FINAL VIEW

2nd Lieutenant J.D. Sinclair describes the Somme battlefields in the closing months of the war

The two weeks I have been out here seem like two months. I suppose it is because I have done such a lot during that time.

On my way up to the line I passed through Amiens and the old Somme battlefields. The former has been badly shattered. Luckily, the Cathedral has escaped damage, and the people are just beginning to return.

The Somme battlefields are a wide expanse of utter desolation where the very trees have been killed; they stand like gaunt spectres sorrowing over the once peaceful and beautiful country.

The school magazine, December 1918

Two

IN THOSE FLYING MACHINES

War broke out in 1914, just five years after Louis Blériot had made the first cross-Channel flight. The new skills of flying had all the excitement and glamour for adventurous young men – especially as these early flying machines were still precariously experimental.

Bournemouth had been the scene of Britain's very first air casualty, when Charles Rolls (of Rolls-Royce fame) had been killed there when his aircraft spectacularly crashed during an early air show.

All Tig's boys would have known of this, and perhaps some had even witnessed this first air disaster. Nevertheless, the temptation to join the newly formed Royal Flying Corps or the Royal Naval Air Service proved irresistible.

2nd Lieutenant E.J.H. Douch has a narrow escape

I have done 15 hours' flying in the last three days... I have had some adventure since my last letter, which resulted in my pilot going home to 'Blighty.' He is a South African and a very good fellow, as well as an excellent pilot.

It happened last Sunday, when we were on an artillery patrol. The pilot was dropping bombs on some Hun transport and I was very much interested in a Hun battery, which I intended to strafe.

Suddenly I heard – pop – pop – pop!! behind us. I jumped up and saw a Hun [aeroplane] driving at us. He only fired about 30 rounds and then sheered off. I had three jams with my gun in ten rounds! The pilot got two in his leg and he temporarily lost control, so we did a merry dive for three thousand feet.

I did not know he was wounded, but thought the controls were shot through. We got one through the petrol tank, just in front of me. Luckily he retained presence of mind enough to switch the engine off so it couldn't catch on fire. He brought the machine back and made a 'topping' landing at an aerodrome.

Then I discovered he was wounded and his seat was full of blood. The old 'bus was a picture, full of bullet holes. I mean to get even some day, though!

The school magazine, December 1916

2nd Lieutenant Douch manages another escape

A few days ago I was ranging a battery on a trench, and both my pilot and I were feeling tremendously bucked with life. We were both singing ragtime, and he was rocking the machine in time to it, when we saw a machine from our squadron doing a very steep spiral. We thought the pilot was also suffering from an attack of joie de vivre. Then I turned round to look behind us, when I saw a nasty looking black Hun with huge black crosses, just turning to attack us.

I got the gun working, and got him on the turn, which put the wind up him somewhat. So he dived past and then another came up. I got this one also on the turn. In all, three machines came for us, and the sky seemed full of Huns, as they were tremendously fast and absolutely made rings round us.

Then, horrors ! A machine dived straight at us and at the same time the gun jammed badly. Before I could get it to work again I had to take off the drum, free the cartridges which had got jammed in the feed, and put on another drum. Happily his gun seemed to jam also, for I only heard about five rounds fired.

After diving I put several rounds into him and I feel sure I 'pinked' him, for he dived sideways on one wing, and then I lost sight of him.

We only had a single bullet through the machine, though the Huns were at one time within ten yards of our tail, and I have no doubt this happy result was due to the skill of my pilot, who made several sharp turns. In all, four machines were attacked about the same time. One fellow got caught, and the pilot was shot through the lungs.

The observer brought the machine safely down, but the poor pilot died the same day. He had only been with us a week, but had served all through the Gallipoli Campaign.

The school magazine, December 1916

Aircraftsman C.V.B. Botham praises the modern seaplane

We are getting ready what I think will turn out to be a few surprises for the Germans this summer. Although the weather is so rough and severe there is still a fair amount of flying done, as it is essential that the various patrols are done if there is the slightest hope of the machine and pilot standing the weather, and it is very surprising how steady the modern seaplane is even in exceedingly rough weather.

The school magazine, April 1917

Norman Wragg and the Boche aeroplanes

... we had spent three weeks in the, at that time, most active part of the line, in fact we saw some fairly heavy fighting.

The Boche aeroplanes, strange to say, were our chief trouble. I think they had their 'travelling circus' (about 20 of their best fliers with their best machines) in front of us. However, when we left the line, that 20 had dwindled somewhat.

The last experience we saw of them was as we came out, one of the Boche aeroplanes got about four miles behind our front line and brought down a couple of our observation balloons. Then, when the observers had jumped out with parachutes and were descending, help-less in the air, the wretched Hun dived on them and fired on them with his machine gun.

The school magazine, July 1917

L.D.R. Sturmer has just joined the Royal Flying Corps

I am writing to let you know that I am under canvas. [He is writing from the RFC Depot Camp, South Farnborough]

I enlisted... and found myself in the Royal Flying Corps. After pre-liminary training in drill and camp life men are drafted from here to squadrons of the RFC at home or abroad.

Young men joining the Army might do worse than apply at the Polytechnic, Regent Street, for enlistment in the RFC. The staff is large enough to avoid the delays which seem inseparable from so many recruiting offices. The pay is 2s per day for a second air-mechanic (equivalent to private), and the conditions down here as regards sanita-tion, discipline and quality of food are first rate.

If a recruit is fit for general service he may enter as fitter, carpen-ter, electrician, rigger, cook, coppersmith, shorthand typist, etc., etc. Otherwise he will be employed as storekeeper, officer's servant, etc.

Many men are drafted there from this camp, and also to the Royal Air Park close by. Detachments leave almost daily for France or Egypt. About one in 50 or so goes up in the air in balloon or machine, I believe, but there is always a possibility of having the closest dealings with these wonderful biplanes which flit continually over our camp, banking to the perpendicular, or looping.

I hope my draft will be to Egypt. I will let you know where it happens to be.

The school magazine, July 1916

L.D.R. Sturmer gets a joy-ride in a Maurice Farman Biplane

The last time I wrote to you was from Farnborough. Before leaving, I was successful in obtaining a flight.

A nervous joy it was on getting the promise of a flight, a hope on having it postponed, and a real joy on being seated behind the pilot in a Maurice Farman Biplane.

He rose smoothly, circled by Lee, over the Solent, towards Portsmouth. The spirals, swoops and nose-dives were very exhilarating. The air went down my ears so that I could hear it for days afterwards, but we weren't up more than 20 minutes, and it was a fine evening [11 September].

At 4,000 feet (given by a mechanic as being a pilot's estimate) the earth rose up in front and went over my head. It was an upright 'bank'. I was strapped across the waist, but was told not to hang on at all. This was the only surprise: the rest was plain sailing, with a splendid living map spread below, showing the whole of Southampton Water, half the Isle of Wight, and beyond Portsmouth Harbour.

The pilot came very low over Portsmouth Harbour, and the wind being easterly we 'stunted' often [made no progress].

The school magazine, December 1916

2nd Lieutenant E.J.H. Douch with aircraft in the mud

Attempting to walk in thick Somme mud anything over six inches deep is not at all pleasant. Walking on duck-boards is quite an art, and one soon acquires quite a nautical roll, known as 'the duckboard glide.'

THE FARMAN BROTHERS

Sturmer's joy-ride in a 'Maurice Farman Biplane' is a reminder of the famous aviation pioneers, the brothers Henry and Maurice Farman, who hold an important place in the early history of aircraft development and manufacture.

Their father was an English journalist who had settled in Paris, so although they had a French nationality and upbringing, they also had a British background. Henry (Henri) (1874–1958) was the elder, and he became famous for setting early records for various flights – for example, he flew the first one-kilometre circuit in France, on January 13 1908.

Maurice, the younger brother (1877–1964) was keen on designing and constructing aeroplanes, and together the two brothers opened an aircraft factory in 1912 at Boulogne-sur-Seine, where they produced their biplanes.

The brothers produced many different models, and Sturmer's joy-ride must have filled him with immense pride, having experienced the cutting-edge of aviation technology.

After the war, the Farman brothers built the first 'long-distance' passenger plane, *The Goliath*, which began its regular Paris to London passenger flights in February 1919.

The Flight Commander decided that it would be impossible to get the machines out of the sheds, on account of the sea of mud. Therefore a road had to be made, and P – and I were selected to forage for broken bricks to make a suitable foundation.

We collected a three-ton lorry and wended our way to a farm, about half a mile off. Here we knew was the remains of an old barn, only two walls of which were standing. An attempt was first made to dislodge the bricks one by one, but that is a terribly slow method of filling a three-ton lorry. We then set to work to pull down a good portion of the wall. It fell with a tremendous crash, and all set to work loading.

Soon a very irate French farmer came up and in French asked P
– why we were pulling down his cow-shed. P – is decidedly not a
French scholar, and as he did not 'comprong' he appealed to me to
pacify the farmer.

I explained, in my best French, that he could take it on quite good
authority that 'l'armée anglaise' would repay him in time. Even that
would not pacify him, so I referred him to the 'Chief of the Squadron.'
I gathered he went there afterwards, as there was the inevitable
inquiry, and the matter was settled by the 'armée anglaise' paying him
seventy-five centimes. The bricks were carted back to the aerodrome,
and the rest of the morning was spent in carrying ashes, provided by
the beneficent REs, to the scene of operations.

After lunch, owing to the success of our expedition in the morning,
P – and I were again sent to go for a forage round an aerodrome not far
distant, which had just been vacated. So another lorry was chartered,
and we drove to the aerodrome, to find two 'Poilus' in possession.
['Poilu' was a slang word for a French army private. Literally, it means
'hairy'.] However, a chat and five francs worked wonders, and we were
given 'carte blanche' to take what we wanted. The former occupants
had left nothing of much use, except duckboards, with which we
loaded the lorry, and departed home.

Next morning more work awaited us. We went down to the aerodrome to find that after the heavy rain during the night the inside of
the shed resembled an indoor swimming bath. That meant trenches
had to be dug to conduct the water into more decorous paths.

Each officer was allotted a section of the proposed trench, and
after a period of very strenuous labour, when the water was let
in, it was found that the depth varied directly as the energy of the
respective workers. In order to make the water overcome its natu-
ral disinclination to run up hill, the officers had to go in single file
down the trench pushing the unwilling fluid with a piece of board.
An edifying spectacle!

Then to a good wash and lunch, with the prospect of a pleasant,
slack afternoon. This was soon shattered, however, by the appearance

of a messenger with the doleful tidings that the clouds were breaking and flying was possible...

... a hurried lunch is eaten, and the air soon resounds with the roar of the machines on which the ever-popular game of 'Strafing the Hun' is played.

The school magazine, April 1917

Wireless operator Walter Cutland and 'spotting' planes

Wireless work plays a tremendously important part in the warfare on the Western Front. All the 'spotting' is done by specially fitted planes, which work in connection with the batteries at which our wireless operators are stationed. This necessitates a thorough training being given to the pilots in aerial observation and wireless work – principally sending and receiving of Morse code.

The school magazine, July 1917

2nd Lieutenant H.L. Holland survives a mid-air collision

2nd Lieutenant H.L. Holland, RFC, was in collision a few months ago with another aeroplane. At the time of the accident both machines were travelling at about 70 miles an hour. It is not surprising that the 'planes' were wrecked beyond repair, but – wonderful to relate – both pilots escaped with a severe shaking.

Dr Fenwick, writing in the school magazine, April 1918

Lieutenant H.L. Le Roy is shot down and becomes a prisoner of war

Lieutenant H.L. Le Roy was taken prisoner on May 22nd [1918] on returning from a night bombing raid.

It appears that, after dropping his 'pills' (as he calls them) on the objective, he lost his direction on the way back. The enemy anti-aircraft guns, which had been very persistent throughout the whole of the raid, followed him in his flight, and at last managed to knock out one of his engines. The aeroplane was thus brought down and the occupants – Le Roy (the pilot), his observer, and a 'rating' – made prisoners, fortunately unhurt.

He was taken first to Karlsruhe, then to Landshut (Bavaria), and finally to Stralsund. Apart from the delay in receiving parcels of food and clothing, and the hardship which that involved, Le Roy's letters indicate that he has not been badly treated and that he has kept in good health and spirits.

Dr Fenwick, writing in the school magazine, December 1918

2nd Lieutenant J. H.A. Porter manages to avoid getting into 'the hands of the huns'

J.H.A. Porter (2nd Lieutenant, RAF) was flying over Metz in his Handley-Page, and dropping bombs there. The Huns turned the searchlights and anti-aircraft guns on his machine, killing the observer and one of the gunners, and putting one engine out of order. He had just enough petrol left to pilot the machine and land it three miles this side of Switzerland. It was 3 a.m., and at first he thought that he and his party were in the hands of the Huns, but was greatly relieved to find that they were with the Czechs and therefore safe.

Two days afterwards he was sent home with shaken nerves to Swanage RAF Hospital. Before this he had been for seven weeks night flying and bomb-dropping.

Dr Fenwick, writing in the school magazine, December 1918

When Dr Fenwick wrote this in December 1918, the RAF was only nine months old, having changed from being merely the Royal Flying Corps – which was still a part of the army.

It's interesting to note that the ranks of the officers in Dr Fenwick's reports are still army ones – the RAF hadn't yet invented its own hierarchy of ranks, such as 'Pilot Officer', 'Flying Officer' and 'Squadron Leader'.

Lieutenant R.H. Peck, 'nose downwards, in a straight plunge'

Lieut. R.H. Peck, attached to the Royal Flying Corps, had a thrilling time as the observer in an aeroplane flight made some time ago over the German lines in Flanders. The following account is extracted from a newspaper cutting: –

'The pilot flew low so that his observer might see something worth while for his note-book - too low, so that suddenly, out of a burst of shrapnel, a jagged piece of shell touched the pilot's leg.

Such a touch is enough to cut off a limb. The young officer believed his leg was almost severed, and although it was not quite so bad as that, he lost control of his machine, and, for a moment or two, of all his senses.

He was over 7,000 feet high, and the aeroplane fell, nose downwards, in a straight plunge. The observer clung to the gun, which was slipping from its straps. The drums which hold the cartridges had already scattered to earth. The crash would come in a second or two.

But the flight officer had got a new grip upon his consciousness and steering-geer. In spite of his loss of blood and that momentary swoon, he not only brought his machine up to level planes, but flew steadily back above the enemy's lines and above their storm of shrapnel, until after a journey of no less than thirty-five minutes he made an unbungled landing in an aerodrome. Here he sat in his saddle, afraid to move lest his leg should fall off, and he remained in his place until the doctors rescued him and carried him away to the hospital.

There he still lies, and there is hope that his leg may be saved [But see next entry.]

The school magazine, December 1916

Lieutenant R.H. Peck meets his death – shot down in Mesopotamia

Roland Peck... was the pilot of a Henri Farman biplane reconnoitring over the Turkish lines, below Kut-el-Amara, Captain W.G. Palmer being the observer.

The aeroplane was brought down by the enemy's gunfire, and both of the officers were killed instantaneously.

The enemy aviators dropped a message in our lines informing us of the fate of the two officers, and stating that this was the fortune of war.

The loss of your son was greatly regretted by all ranks of the RFC; during his short period of service in Mesopotamia he had shown himself to be a competent and gallant pilot.

Lieutenant Peck's Commanding Officer, quoted in the school magazine,
December 1916

2nd Lieutenant E.J.H. Douch puts 'the wind up the poor Huns'

After the attack I went back to my shoot, and put the wind up the poor Huns in the trenches, for they kept on sending up rockets as a signal for their own artillery to send up some stuff in retaliation. So we let them know that we didn't care for their aeroplanes...

The school magazine, December 1916

Lieutenant C.J. Sims brings down two machines

Lieutenant C. J. Sims (RAF) has been awarded the DFC (Distinguished Flying Cross). His Captain writes: 'Your son thoroughly earned his distinction. He is a splendid fellow and quite one of our best pilots, as well as being exceptionally keen on his work. We are all proud of him.' (So are all Bournemouthians.)

Sims is the 'baby' of his squadron, but managed to bring down two enemy machines in his first three months, an exceptional performance.

Dr Fenwick, writing in the school magazine, December 1918

Three

AROUND THE WORLD

INDIA

Brian New is sent to India via the Suez Canal

We were packed away in the front portion of the ship, and 1,500 men had to occupy a space which only a hundred or so could do with any degree of comfort. At meal times we had to descend into our quarters and partake of our food in semi-darkness. The mid-day meal was quite good, only it was served up in a very distasteful manner, and the atmosphere below, as time passed, became almost unbearable...

We stayed five days at Port Said, but only the officers landed, and from what they told me Port Suez is a very dirty place.

By this time the heat was affecting us, and many men fainted, but in the Red Sea conditions became worse. One day I was told the temperature was 110 degrees in the shade. It was impossible to do any drill, and it required courage to descend to get our meals. Of course, most of us slept on deck, but I believe a few braved the foul conditions below. To make things worse, we were inoculated and vaccinated; fortunately neither had any distressing effect on me, but some of the poor fellows had a very rough time.

Nothing eventful took place on the voyage across the Indian Ocean, and we landed at Bombay on November 10th, having been on the water since October 9th.

...We spent two months in Bombay, and we are now at Meerut for real training, for climatic conditions here are more favourable for strenuous work. The first three days were very cold, with frost each morning, and we were issued thick woollen sweaters. It rained solidly Sunday and Monday, but now again it is clear and cold, with sunshine all day.

Meerut is purely a military centre, but is quite historical. It was here that the Mutiny broke out, and we attend the same church as did the soldiers in those days. The Mutiny broke out while our soldiers were in church, and of course, unarmed, and as they came out they were shot down like rabbits. A shot fired by the mutineers went right through the clock in the tower, and since then the clock has not been touched, and the time it stopped at was 11.35 a.m.. Since the Mutiny every soldier has to carry his rifle and twenty rounds of ball ammunition with him to church.

The school magazine, March 1915

2nd Lieutenant B.B. New returned to serve in France, where he was killed in action on 17 August 1917, aged 26.

THE DARDANELLES

Captain Hands lives on bully-beef for over a fortnight

I thought that an account of life in the Dardanelles might interest you. I left England in June [1915] and came straight out, the only stop being one at Alexandria of two days.

I was fortunate enough to get ashore, and found the place most interesting, especially the Arab towns, where the natives keep their animals in the house and the road is full of straying cows, dogs, hens, etc.

Life is very strenuous on the Peninsula, as it is very hilly indeed, and by the time one has spent one's day clambering up slopes and being sniped at periodically, memories of some of the flatter parts of England come back rather forcefully.

We all live in dug-outs here, and one's comfort varies directly as the length of time spent in the same place. I had a lot of moving a fortnight ago, and as I had to dig myself in at a different place practically every day it was not worth while to build an imposing place.

I have now been stationary for a week and live in quite a handsome erection, proof against bullets and shrapnel, which is rather an advantage in these times. Food here is plentiful enough, but is apt to be monotonous. I have been living on bully-beef for over a fortnight now.

The school magazine, December 1915

SALONICA (THESSALONIKA)

Private Donald Spickernell works in the Medical Corps with 66 Field Ambulance – not an easy safe time

After a spell in France, where we saw plenty of active work, we came out here during November, 1915. We were in the Serbian retirement of December, and are now doing advanced dressing station duties among the troops here. We have thus had many exciting times since leaving England.

Have slept in all sorts of strange places: at the roadside, in fields, in dug-outs, in barns, and even under an old wooden railway station platform!

Some people think we have a very easy safe time, but such is often far from so.

The school magazine, July 1916

INDIA

Harold Bott is not reconciled to his fate having been sent to Bangalore

Little did I think, when I wrote you on joining up that two years hence I should be helping to guard King George's interests in India. But Tommies cannot be choosers, Sir, and the War Office wind blows us wherever it likes.

When it blew us here I am afraid we did not come with a very good heart, as a few days before leaving England we had orders for France, which were cancelled at the last moment.

We have never become reconciled to our fate. The people of Bangalore – chiefly Eurasians – keep very much aloof from us, and we are left to our own devices when we have finished our morning parade at 12. Most of our spare time we fill up with sports – football, cricket, hockey, tennis.

We have done a lot of musketry since coming here, both range and field firing... We are not in India for garrison duty, but are being trained as a Brigade for active service. We hope to be in at the death.

When I am on guard and pickets and similar dreary jobs, my mind often reverts to England, and I often wonder how the old school is getting on. I read with great regret of the death of Mr Atkin and Mr Forman and several old boys I knew, on the battlefield, and with pride of the distinctions won by old boys in the field. Especially was I interested in the account of Captain Drayton's winning of the Military Cross, as he was an old friend of mine who went through the school with me.

The school magazine, December 1916

CEYLON (SRI LANKA)

A.G. Ridley has a pukka rebellion all to himself

We have just been having stirring times – had a Pukka rebellion all to ourselves.

Things are quiet now. Martial Law still prevails and the streets after 7 p.m. are as quiet as the grave. Everyone is in uniform, day and night: meanwhile between duties we are trying to carry on business, which is very flat and more or less at a standstill.

The Ceylonese have been the disturbers. They took the opportunity to show their displeasure at a court order at Gampola, which ruled that the Moormen – shopkeepers – had a right to monopolise a certain street for their particular boutiques (shops). This they did at their festival Wesak (Buddha's birthday) by turning out the Moormen, pillaging and looting the boutiques, and setting fire to them, and setting on to the Moormen and women – knifing and killing many of both.

From Gampola the trouble spread all over the island in a very short time, exactly the same happening in every place – killing, looting, and burning. Thousands of Moors fled daily to India, leaving their bungalows, etc., at the mercy of the rabble. Colombo broke out three weeks last Monday, and we were all called out on the Tuesday. Not a soul to be seen in the stores – every European rushed to the Armoury and got rifle, bayonet and ammunition, and fell in at the Barrack Square, not knowing what was going to happen next...

The next day Martial Law was declared, and then they had their lesson. We raided the native quarters and made a house-to-house search for arms, knives, and all iron implements and weapons. Wherever we found a Ceylonese house or shop shut up we broke down the shutters and ransacked the place.

We had instructions to shoot any who showed the least resistance.

The school magazine, July 1915

BRITISH CONSULATE, SYRA
(SYROS, GREEK ISLAND)

G.H. Mate, in an important reserved occupation,
feels an 'outcast' because he is not in Flanders

You may know that we at Syra here have a Consular District comprising 'the Islands of the Greek Archipelago' (and they are legion!), and just previous to the outbreak of hostilities we had the Islands, formerly Turkish, of Mitylene, Chios, and Samos tacked on. In consequence, apart from ordinary peace routine work, the extraordinary work entailed by hostilities has been double, in addition to which I had, last year, to organise an efficient Intelligence Department here for the whole district to cope with enemy activities.

For this, I was specially fitted by my knowledge of modern Greek and – what is of even more importance, perhaps – a first hand acquaintance of the wily Greek himself – whom to 'get around' you must meet on his own ground with his own weapons...

All this you will appreciate has weighed with me, and has been my reason for not throwing everything up and coming home to join up... I have been twice told that I am essential where I am, and reflect on results achieved and work put through – in great part thanks to my acquaintance with the local language – on acquaintance possessed by no other Consular Officer in the district – I am forced to the conclusion that I must stay here.

I know that just now everybody in England has but poor thoughts for those who shelter themselves in reserved occupations and beneath the Government umbrella, and this must be my excuse for the foregoing. It is hard to feel one is an 'outcast' when one has every reason to believe that one is rendering better service than would perhaps one rifle more in Flanders.

The school magazine, December 1916

SALONICA (THESSALONIKA)

H.J. Finch describes Salonica and finds some captured German ammunition

[During the First World War, from 1915–18, Salonica (Thessalonika) was the headquarters of the allied armies in the East. It is the second largest town and port in Greece.]

At the town [Salonica] the smell is fearful and I tremble to think of what it is like in hot weather. Every nation under heaven seems to be represented in the population, refugees, Turks, Greeks, all in native costume or costumes showing a ridiculous blend of European and native. For instance, baggy red trousers and an English coat, or full native rig and a cast-off uniform cap. As for the military, there is every conceivable type of uniform of all our Allies. For money you get change for a sixpence in a mixture of French, Greek, Spanish, and English coins. The whole place is a glorious Irish stew of smells, foreign peoples, mules, mud and gorgeous uniforms.

While working on this ammunition dump we came across some cases of captured German 4.2 inch shells, made for the Bulgar and obviously got up for effect. The wooden cases were metal lined and the finish of the shells far superior to ours.

But – the driving charge is too small and the bursting charge ridiculously inadequate. One of ours of the same size contains twice the amount of explosive, so the ordnance sergeant said. So there again the German indulges in extensive 'window dressing.'

It is surprising how little there is here – we might have arrived but yesterday. Every fragment of paper, every scrap of waste is burnt. You should see how stables, etc., have been constructed out of empty petrol tins cut open and flattened out.

The school magazine, April 1917

CHRISTMAS IN MESOPOTAMIA, 1916

C.E. Hyam enjoys a Christmas dinner in a dug-out

I had my Christmas dinner in a dug-out in one of the redoubts, but nevertheless I collected a very good 'spread' for myself. The only drawback was that I was unable to procure a turkey – this was not surprising, seeing there were none to be got – and so a boiled duck had to do instead.

However, the time-honoured plum pudding was at hand. The men were given 50 cigarettes, a pint of beer, and ½lb of Christmas pudding each, whilst my Company Commander distributed tinned peas, beans, and sherry to the men under his command.

The school magazine, April 1917

INDIA

2nd Lieutenant J.J. Gossling goes crawling and scrambling

I had to go to join my unit at Bangalore. Well, I arrived at Bangalore to find the regiment gone north... I arrived at a place called Burham, where the regiment had encamped for annual manoeuvres.

It was a small plot of ground between two ranges of hills, simply full of dust, which got well stirred up when we were on the march. It was also bitterly cold and generally a miserable spot to be in.

We had three months crawling and scrambling on the hills (called mountain warfare by the higher powers) and were heartily glad to leave for our hill station near Simla, a place called Dagshai.

The school magazine, July 1917

MESOPOTAMIA (BASRA IN IRAQ)

C.E. Hyam describes the mixed population in 'Busra'

I am at present figuring in a new capacity, namely, that of cipher officer in the Adjutant-General's office.

Busra is a very cosmopolitan town, for amongst its inhabitants are Arabs, Persians, Armenians, Turks, Syrians, Chinese, Japanese, West Indians, Indians, and British.

... the Arab is usually of fine physique, brave, intelligent, and extremely generous. The Arabs are very strong men, but they are not so powerful as the Kurds, who are short, thick set fellows with long hair and closely-fitting skull caps. These people can carry loads of stuff on their backs. I myself have seen one bearing fifteen boxes on his back.

The Arab has no home life and he seems to spend all his spare time lounging about in coffee shops, which are always packed all day.

The school magazine, July 1917

'HORMUZ ISLE'

Lieutenant C.C.T. Osborne is Medical Officer and 'King'

Here I am, 'King of Hormuz Isle.' I brought my company across here on Wednesday to do some quarrying work. I'm the only European on the Island, so you see I'm like Robinson Crusoe. The only difference is that Crusoe only had one companion, whom he called 'Friday,' but I've got about 300 black men as companions. With the exception of about 30 or 40 Persians, whom I'm also employing, the Island was deserted.

In addition to my other duties I am also Medical Officer (tips?). They've given me three kinds of medicine – quinine, castor oil, and Epsom salts, so I dispense it as follows: the first day a man comes sick I give him a dose of quinine, if he comes the second day he gets castor oil, and the third day's treatment is naturally Epsom salts.

The funny part is I hardly know the difference between fever and whooping cough, or diarrhoea and toothache. One comfort, the men here don't know my qualifications as an MD.

The school magazine, December 1918

THE GREEK ISLAND OF SYROS

G.H. Mate, Vice-Consul, Syra, Greece, eats stale bread

G.H. Mate, Vice-Consul, Syra, Greece, sheds a lurid light on conditions there.

'We still have the bread famine,' he says, 'and I fancy that it is pretty nearly as bad throughout Greece, although not so bad on the mainland as here. I have not tasted bread for about five days, except a bit a neighbour luckier than us gave us, and a bit I found stale as the hills in a cupboard.'

Dr Fenwick, writing in the school magazine, December 1915

ALEXANDRIA, EGYPT

R.V. Montgomery, in the Motor Ambulance Corps, has just been transferred from Salonica to Egypt

The roads in Salonica are very bad, although they are always being repaired. We used to get some 'rude awakenings' with enemy aeroplanes, but fortunately they did not favour us with bombs! They used to get a very hot reception!

The town itself is very pretty to look at from the harbour, lying as it does on the slope, but like most other Eastern places, with the exception of a street or so, is not too clean.

Early in May [1916] all Field Ambulance cars were called in and... we had a fine voyage here [Egypt], as there were only about 30 of us on board – the rest came after – we just missed seeing that 'Zepp.' brought down [Zeppelin].

We were at the Depôt here for a month, and then were sent here, about eight miles from the town itself, called 'Sidi Beshr' Camp.

There are two of us and we have Ford ambulances, and do all running about for the Camp Commandant, etc., in connection with the camp itself and also the new rest camp, where the troops are sent for seven days' rest. They have a very good time with no parades, etc. Concerts are given most evenings; there is also a YMCA and a Cinema. They have a pass for the town.

We are very comfortable, and can hardly call it 'active service' although it gets very monotonous, as one of us has always to be on duty.

The school magazine, July 1916

SALONICA (THESSALONIKA)

A.J.A. Kerr describes Salonica and has a 'Taube' over him

After disembarking we had a long march, and the main characteristic of the road was dirt, dust and questionably clean humanity, but the most important of these was dust – dust so thick that you could not see more than half-a-dozen yards in front of you.

In the town, no decent shops, plenty of dirt, smell and donkeys with only head and tail on view, the rest hidden by packs, on the top of the aforesaid very small donkey and pack a very dirty man, smoking the inevitable cigarettes.

We had a good experience our first day on shore, having a 'Taube' over us and the anti-guns going 'pop' all over the show.

The school magazine, December 1916

A 'Taube' was an early German monoplane – literally meaning 'dove', from its bird-like shape.

MESOPOTAMIA

2nd Lieutenant Cedric Swallow finds his chatties are frozen over

I landed at Basra on October 2nd [1916] and spent a few days at Asher Barracks, where we handed our draft over, five of us brought out 235 men.

We came on up on the Tigris to Sheikh Saad, where we were doing defence work. We are now a little nearer to the line; still on L. of C. work. I expect you have already hard all about this country from others, and my impressions agree entirely with all that has been said and written about it. It is an uninteresting, unhealthy place, of no commercial use to anyone as it exists at present, though I believe much could be done here.

This is, fortunately for me, the best time of the year here; the heat at midday is quite comfortable, my arms and legs are already quite bronzed, but the nights are bitterly cold. I found our water chatties [earthenware water-pots] frozen over this morning! I have been quite fit so far with the exception of a fortnight's sickness due to sandfly fever.

The school magazine, April 1917

EGYPT

Lieutenant A. Whitting captures chameleons, scorpions and tarantulas

I have made a move once more and am now in the land of milk and honey, so-called, I should think, by the complete absence of both delicacies.

I find this country very different from Macedonia. It is much hotter here, and there are a tremendous number of flies, but we do not get the unpleasant smells which were so prevalent in the former country.

This place is entirely uninhabited all the way east of the Suez Canal, being one large waste of sand, with a dried-up river bed running through it. I understand this floods in the rainy season, the river rising to over ten feet.

Every morning at about 11.30 a strong breeze springs up, which makes the heat more bearable, but, on the other hand, blows all sand and dust everywhere. The consequence is we get a good deal of sand in our food, and one has to cover everything up which is not in immediate use. Otherwise we get a fairly good time, although everyone has his little 'grouse'.

At present things are fairly quiet in that portion of the line we are holding, but I think we all hope we shall get a chance of 'pushing' in the near future.

We see many weird reptiles and insects here. I have caught many chameleons, scorpions and tarantulas. The first-named is rather a delightful little thing and can see in every direction, each eye being independent of the other.

The water is the chief trouble. It has to be brought to us in fanati's [?] on camels, so we are limited to a certain ration by day. As a rule when it does arrive it is warm, so we seldom get a cool drink, except when ice is procurable.

The school magazine, December 1917

BAGHDAD

Frank Lawrence gives a detailed description of Baghdad as it was in 1918

Leaving Basrah, I travelled by train to Amara, which is beautifully situated in a palm grove and is supposed to be near the Garden of Eden. From this town I went by river steamer to Kut, where General Townshend and the garrison were compelled to surrender to the Turks on April 29, 1916.

From Kut I travelled by rail to Baghdad, having taken five days to do the whole journey of about five hundred miles. Like all Eastern cities, Baghdad, with its big white buildings all along the river front, looks a fine city as one approaches; but on closer investigation it proves to have many narrow, filthy, smelly streets. Hundreds of houses, many streets, and several bazaars were destroyed to allow a broad thoroughfare like New Street to be made. But it was done, and it has its trams and electric light like any modern city now.

But Baghdad as we know it retains but little to suggest the city in its prime. Though even now of no mean importance, the present city is but a melancholy reminder of a vast metropolis which included within its limits the now detached suburb of Muadham. It was replete with gardens and palaces, and in the Middle Ages was indisputably the second city of the world, Constantinople (Stamboul) being the first.

For a time, Baghdad ranked first as a centre of culture and education. The origin of the settlement which was to become the fairy city of the Arabian Nights is shrouded in obscurity. Only as recently as 1848 did it become known, through the discoveries of Sir Henry Rawlingson, that a city probably existed here in Babylonian times. Bricks bearing the name, titles, and conquests of Nebuchadnezzar II (605–562 BC) were unearthed on the right bank of the Tigris above the present North Bridge.

The population of Baghdad just before the war was about 250,000. Chief among the nationalities represented are the Arabs and Persians, with a few Turks, Kurds, and Indians. But every day one hears many languages spoken in the bazaars – Kurdish, Armenian, French, English, Arabic, Persian, and Hindustani.

Two-thirds of this population are of the Mohammedan religion. Of the remainder, fifty thousand are Jews and nine thousand are Christians. The latter are of several sects and denominations.

The dress of most Arabs and Persians, and of a number of Christians and Jews, consists of a cotton shirt and drawers, over which is worn a long tunic (zibun) and an outdoor garment called an 'aba,' or cloak, made of dark coloured wool, cotton, or silk. The richer classes carrying one hand a string of amber beads.

It is by the head-dress chiefly that one is able to distinguish the different peoples. The Arabs of the desert who visit the city, and some of the inhabitants [wear] a large headkerchief with a coil of hair rope wrapped on top.

The town Arabs wear either a plain fez or a coloured skull-cap wrapped round with a long piece of turban cloth. Some of the better classes dress in European style, generally with a fez. Sunni Seyyids (those who claim direct descent from Mohammed) wear a green turban.

From its earliest days the position of Baghdad on the Tigris River and twenty-four miles from the Euphrates River has made it the great trading centre of Eastern Arabia, Mesopotamia, the country above Mosul, and much of Western Persia.

In modern times it has never had any important factories, though it manufactures silk, clothing, and belts. It has, however, been the collecting and distributing point for the very large commerce of these parts.

The finest buildings are the Government Offices, the churches, and the mosques. Of these the Mosque of Khadimain, with its two domes and four large minarets, all overlaid with gold plates claimed to be a quarter of an inch thick, is perhaps the most magnificent in all Mesopotamia. It is a sacred shrine and the chief Shiah mosque in the neighbourhood of Baghdad.

During the British occupation many improvements have been made, and at the present rate of progress Baghdad promises to become as important and wealthy a city as it was in the Middle Ages.

The school magazine, March 1919

Mr Frank Lawrence, who wrote the above description of Baghdad, was a long-serving master at Bournemouth School. He was appointed in April 1914 as a young man – probably his first job. At the declaration of war he tried to join up, but because of poor eyesight, he was initially 'certified to be physically unfit for military service'.

He persisted, however, and in 1917 he was accepted, in Dr Fenwick's words, to 'join the Colours'. He was then sent to Mesopotamia.

He is remembered at Bournemouth School for founding the school Scout Troop shortly after he joined the school in 1914. When he returned after the First World War he and his wife ran the Scout Troop and the Cub Scouts right up until the Second World War.

He finally retired in 1951 – and in 2010 several old retired members of staff could still remember him.

IN THE 'JOLLY OLD MEDITERRANEAN'

Lieutenant J. K. Nethercoate is torpedoed – but lands in Malta in a Naval stoker's pants

You will not be surprised to hear that we were torpedoed by a hostile submarine, but as I managed to keep my head and to maintain my reputation for good luck, I am here with only a few bruises and a contented smile, while as to my kit, it is lying at the bottom of the jolly old Mediterranean!

I was playing bridge in the smoke room and had just called "Two Torpedoes" (i.e. no trumps), when a torpedo struck the boat. I felt a pain in my right shin but it turned out afterwards to be merely a graze.

I got into a boat and as there was only one other officer, who happened to be my junior, I took charge and filled the boat as full as I dared. The sailors lowered away the falls without cutting the life lines, a foolish thing to do, and, as we had a narrow escape from breaking away, I snatched a knife and cut away the lashings, but not before one poor chap had been crushed between the ship and our boat.

I thanked my lucky stars that I knew my job and when the men saw that they were as cool as if on parade.

As soon as we were clear of the ship's side, we started to pick up from the water some of the men, one or two of whom had narrow escapes.

Then came the trouble, for there was a sudden crash. Some said it was a mine, others a shell, but I think it was one of the sniper's rifles, which were always kept loaded at the bottom of the boat; anyhow, it blew a big hole in the bottom.

We bailed furiously but it was hopeless, so some who could swim boarded the small rafts that were floating about. Eight men stayed in the boat which, although full of water, would float on account of the water-tight compartments and, telling them to stay where they were, I dived into the water. They called out, 'Good luck, Sir,' and one threw me an oar.

I saw that the only thing to do was to swim to the destroyer, so, holding on to an oar, I took off my clothes, having previously discarded my slippers. I waited while the destroyer went alongside the troopship and took off a lot of the men. She then turned and picked up the remainder of my boat's crew, but by that time I had drifted some distance away.

I swam like fury, but was too far off for them to throw a rope and they could not wait as the submarines were still about. What surprised me most was that I kept quite cool and felt full of confidence, but it was awful to hear men on all sides calling out like lost souls.

As the destroyer passed I called out quite cheerfully, 'Drop us a line when you can,' and a lieutenant called back, 'Stick it, old man, we shall be back soon.'

It was a long time before they did come back, and when at last I saw them coming in my direction I swam to get in their way. It was my last chance as I was getting cramp and had swallowed a lot of water. I had been in the water for two hours, but fortunately it was warm.

I managed to swim within a rope's throw just in time. They threw me a line with a loop and I took it and slipped the loop over my shoulders. I felt a terrible wrench and that is all I remember till I found my stable mate, Williams, the MO bending over me. They said it was a near thing as I should have been cut up by the propellers if I had missed the rope.

I landed in Malta in a naval stoker's pants and vest, and nothing on my feet – a truly funny sight! We were met at the dock gate by Red Cross men dishing out smokes, and were then taken to various hospitals who fixed us up splendidly. I went straight off to bed, had a meal and slept the clock round, for I had had nothing to eat and had not slept for thirty hours!

The school magazine, July 1917

Four

GETTING WOUNDED

fter the Great War, Bournemouth School's magazine listed all those ex-pupils who had been wounded. One asterisk against a name denoted being wounded once; two asterisks for being wounded twice – and there were several with three or even four asterisks. It's astonishing how these young men deliberately went back to the front to receive yet more mutilations. Here are stories told in their own words by some of the lucky ones who survived.

Private A. C. Stagg spends fifteen days in no man's land, wounded and without food

'How much can a man stand?' or rather, I think, I should say, 'How much can the human body stand?' Evidently a great deal, as you will agree after reading what I have to say.

It was on the 1st of July [1916 – the beginning of the Somme offensive] that we had to 'go over the lid.' At 4.30 a.m. we went across. The enemy were shelling us heavily, and, in addition, there was a heavy rifle and machine gun fire.

I hadn't gone far before I was hit, being shot through the chest. I immediately rolled into a shell-hole for better protection, and imagine I lost consciousness for a considerable time. When I came to, I heard a voice, and discovered that there was another fellow in the shell-hole, about 15 yards away, so I decided to join him.

It was while crawling across that I got shot through the arm by a sniper. How long we were in that shell-hole I don't know, but it must have been several days – by then we were parched with thirst, and welcomed the heavy rain which came, and which we collected in our steel helmets. I had thrown off my equipment, and with it went all my food, so that you can imagine that I was feeling a bit hungry, especially as I was weak with my wounds.

All at once the other fellow decided to crawl in, and off he went. That was the last I saw or heard of him.

I decided then that it was impossible to stay out day after day, and started to crawl in myself. I found it an agonising and exhausting job, and have no idea how long it actually took me, but eventually I got into an unused trench. Here I discovered a dug-out, and turned in. All I wanted was rest and oblivion, and I slept – how long I don't know – but I think I must have been unconscious again for some considerable time. In the dug-out I came across a bag containing some bits of army biscuits, and these, soaked in rain water, were all the food I had. I was absolutely too weak to do anything but lie and sleep, and did not move except when I crawled to get water.

To sum matters up, I was hit on the 1st July and discovered on the 15th – meaning to say that for 15 days I was without food (practically) and with my wounds undressed. Thanks to the careful attention and the kindness of the hospital sisters and doctors, my wounds are healing fast, and I hope soon to put on weight again. I certainly ought to, because I am fed here with everything that is nourishing and good.

It was a horrible experience, but I pulled through, and there's a lot of life in the old dog yet.

The school magazine, December 1916

Private Stagg wrote this in a convalescent home near Huddersfield. He had had trench foot, and while he was in hospital in France gangrene was feared. He was shot through the lung, and the bullet came out at the back; shot through the arm; and had seven shrapnel wounds in the thigh. A year previously Private Stagg had been in hospital in Egypt with blood poisoning.

2nd Lieutenant G.E. Hunt gets buried twice

[Dr Fenwick wrote this account, taken from a letter he had received from Hunt, and having seen him when convalescing at the Mont Dore Hospital in Bournemouth – now the Town Hall.]

2nd Lieutenant G.E. Hunt, who left us a year ago and who after obtaining a commission went to France, had there a terrible experience. About 4 o'clock one afternoon he was in a dug-out whilst German shells were flying about and eventually one of them found his position, killed his brother officer and buried him.

This was observed by others who were near, and three of them came to dig him out. They succeeded in getting his head free when another shell burst amongst them and killed all the rescue party.

Hunt received head wounds, was again buried, and this time he lost consciousness, his plight being much worse than before. About three hours later another rescue party came up, dug him out and saved him, and though he had been underground so long, had various wounds, and his hearing was impaired, he is making an excellent recovery and was very cheerful when he came over to see us during his convalescence at the Mont Dore Hospital.

The school magazine, March 1918

E. A. H. Bolton has a 'fine souvenir to bring home'

During the evening of October 21st [1915] our Battalion had the honour of repulsing with heavy loss, a German attack in massed formation.

When I was on sentry in the front line behind Loos, a bullet entered my left shoulder and travelled a few inches down my side. After being bandaged I said I thought I could get back to the hospital without assistance. I knew the way over the top, but not by trench but I hadn't gone 100 yards before the Huns started sending over shrapnel.

I took no notice of this until a shell burst quite close, whereupon I took to the trench. To make matters worse it began to rain. It was about midnight and the trench was filling with water.

Both my arms were wrapped inside my coat, which – owing to my wound – I could not wear in the usual way, and it was quite dark, so I found it very difficult to get along.

After wandering about for an hour, wet through and altogether in a pitiable state, I somehow got in the reserve trench which was occupied by another London Battalion. Explaining my plight to the sentry, he got their stretcher-bearers out of 'bed.' They were jolly decent chaps, and did what they could to ease the pain, taking me to their dressing station where I arrived about 4.30 a.m. absolutely 'done' and quite ready to faint.

However, 'All's well that ends well.' The bullet is a fine souvenir to bring home.

The school magazine, March 1916

Captain Drayton is surrounded by five Germans

When, after a heavy bombardment, the enemy raided our trenches, although wounded, he collected a few men and repulsed all attacks on his portion of the trench. He set a fine example to all around him [Announced 26 June 1916].

It appears that in this case Drayton was dazed and partly buried by a shell explosion. On extricating himself he found that he was surrounded by five Germans, who tried to capture him alive. Drayton shot three of these, and, though wounded by a bullet in the point of the shoulder, he made good his retreat to a neighbouring wood. There he found and rallied some of his men, and, returning with them, recaptured the trench out of which they had just been driven.

Dr Fenwick, writing in the school magazine, July 1916

For this action, 2nd Lieutenant (Temporary Captain) R. Drayton was awarded the Military Cross.

Reginald Fairley is badly wounded and gets captured by 'Saxons'

I had told you in my letters from Germany that it was a grenade that did the damage to my jaw, but that was because the Germans would not allow us to mention explosive bullets. They use them frequently, though they swore they never used such things. But I know what knocked me out.

When I recovered consciousness I had a confused notion of someone talking to me. On looking up I found the trench in front of me was full of Germans, two of whom were covering me with their rifles, while a German corporal told me I had better crawl into the trench if I didn't want another bullet in me.

It was absolutely useless for me to attempt any resistance in my disabled state, so I crawled up to the trench, expecting a bullet for my pains. But to my surprise they were awfully decent to me. Another got out a field dressing and busied himself trying to staunch the blood which literally poured from my throat. Another wiped the blood from my lips, and gave me a drink from his water-bottle. They took off my equipment, and improvised a couple of slings for my arms.

The guard informed me it was well for me that it was a Saxon regiment that had taken me. I was lucky, as I should have had a different reception if it had been a Prussian or Bavarian regiment.

An officer... questioned me as to my regiment, battalion, brigade, and division. To all of which I replied by shaking my head and pointing to my mouth. He cursed at me in German, and told the guard to take me away.

The school magazine, December 1916

Lieutenant M.J. Hellier sees the Lusitania being sunk

Lieut. M.J. Hellier, 6th Shropshire Light Infantry, had a marvellous escape. On November 8th [1914] a bullet pierced one of his arms, then made a surface wound across his chest and emerged after damaging his other arm also.

He returned on the hospital ship *Newhaven* at the same time as the *Anglia*, and had the terrible experience of seeing that and the *Lusitania* go down, feeling that it might be their turn next.

Being wounded in both arms and so unable to swim we can understand what an awful time it must have been. Fortunately no bones were broken, and though the flesh wounds are severe, he is doing wonderfully well. He is now in the Royal Free Hospital (Military Section), Gray's Inn Road, London.

Dr Fenwick, writing in the school magazine, December 1915

THE SINKING OF RMS *LUSITANIA*

The sinking of the *Lusitania* on 7 May 1915 – torpedoed by a German U-boat 11 miles (19 km) off the Old Head of Kinsale, Ireland – was a major event in the early months of the war.

The *Lusitania* was a Cunard luxury ocean liner, with 1,959 people on board when it was attacked by the U-boat. The liner sank in just 18 minutes, killing and drowning 1,198 of its civilian passengers and crew. Naturally, such an unprovoked attack created a huge wave of anti-German feeling around the world.

In particular, the shock-waves of horror were felt in the United States, still a neutral non-participant in the war. The lives of no fewer than 124 US citizens were lost.

This disaster was an important factor in bringing the United States into the war against Germany. However, another two years were to elapse before the actual declaration of war, in April 1917.

Reginald Fairley, now a prisoner, is taken to Dulman Camp, where the food is 'vile'
(a continuation of the previous account on page 87)

The guards tried to make me a bed of sacks in one corner, but I couldn't lie down, as the blood clogged in my throat and I thought I would choke. So I sat with my head in my hands, and never felt so miserable and depressed in all my life, while the blood dripped from my throat to the floor...

After I had been there about an hour a corporal came and said that those who could walk could start for the dressing station behind the firing line, we should have our wounds dressed and be put to bed. So I decided to have a shot for it. We started about 4 p.m. and got beyond the trenches by 6 p.m.

I cannot describe the journey. I was reeling along helped by a man of the Black Watch, who was only slightly wounded. We reached the first station about 6.30, but they would not take me in, but put me in a motor ambulance, and passed two more stations before the one where I was taken in.

When the car stopped I was told to get out; and what a sight I must have been. My trouser leg had been slit up to get at the wound in my leg. I was plastered in mud up over my puttees. When I stepped out of the ambulance I saw a lighted doorway, and just had strength enough to make my way through it.

I had a confused idea of a large room and a group of men in white jackets, then the whole place went round, and I started falling. One of the doctors rushed forward and caught me, and lowered me to the ground. I did not properly lose consciousness, but have a faint recollection of having my clothes cut off me, and of being sponged all over with hot water, and clear bandages being put on my wounds. The doctor squirted some liquid into the wound in my throat, which seemed to freeze it; it was deliciously cool. I was then given a cup of warm soup, and wrapped in a clean white blanket, placed on a stretcher, and carried out into a street.

A few yards down the street we turned into a courtyard, and through a door into a long ward full of white cots, in one of which I was placed, propped up with pillows. The doctor asked me in English if I was comfortable, or was there anything more he could for me. I replied 'No'. but I couldn't thank him enough for what he had done for me.

By his orders my pockets had been emptied, and the contents placed on a little table by my bedside. I thought that ward must have been like heaven, it was so quiet in there, and the bed so clean and soft, and my wounds, now that they were dressed, no longer pained me.

[After this lucky escape from death, Reginald Fairley appears to have been sent to a prisoner-of-war camp at Dulman – but it is not clear where this is.]

The food in Dulman Camp is vile, and the prisoners can do with all the parcels they can get. The parcels arrive safely enough, so no one need be afraid to send them on account of the prisoners not getting them. There is a staff of English sergeants, who receive the parcels from a party of prisoners, who fetch them from the railways in large wagons. These sergeants check them and distribute them, so there is no chance of them going astray.

The school magazine, December 1916

Captain H. A. Short is buried for 45 hours

Captain H. A. Short has returned from France to England, wounded for the fourth time, but is now convalescent. His escape from death seems to have been little short of miraculous. In the great advance at Arras on April 20th [1917], after penetrating about 600 yards behind the German front line, he was hit in the side by a bullet.

He immediately took cover in a neighbouring trench – only to be buried by a German shell. In this condition he remained, inaccessible to rescue owing to the zone of fire, for 45 hours, when a relief party succeeded in reaching him and bringing him in.

The school magazine, July 1917

Dr Fenwick gives a routine account of wounded old boys

H.M. Deans has twice returned wounded from service, and is now at the front for the third time.

W.A. Hodges is also back at the front after recovering from rheumatism and frostbite, sent back to England.

We are glad that the following Old Bournemouthians are recovering satisfactorily: P.R.M. Robertson (who was buried by the explosion of a shell), M.A. Strudwicke (suffering from gas poisoning), H.M. Tollemache (wounded in leg).

We await with great hope and some anxiety further news of D.G. Hazard, who was reported missing [25th May], believed killed.

Dr Fenwick, writing in the school magazine, July 1915

In every school magazine throughout the war, Dr Fenwick gave brief notices such as these, providing scores of accounts of events, wounds, old boys 'missing', and those who had gained military decorations. It must have taken a great deal of his time, as he was constantly in touch with all of them; writing to thank them, encourage them, congratulate them, and sadly, to sympathise with their parents when they were killed.

Lance Corporal E. K. Head gets a glass eye

Lance Corporal E.K. Head was wounded on February 17th [1917] in France, when a piece of shell penetrated his right eye. He was removed to hospital in France, and, later, to the Royal Eye and Ear Hospital, Bradford.

Here, everything possible was done to try and save the eye, but without success, in spite of three operations.

Finally, it became necessary to remove the eye and provide him with an artificial substitute.

The school magazine, July 1917

Lieutenant B.W. Hame MC is knocked out by a 5.9 German shell

He was 'wiring'* in Bourbon Wood during the counter-attack of last November 25th [1917] when a German shell exploded in the middle of a party of eleven men, of whom Hame was one.

He was 'knocked out' and remained unconscious from the shock for several hours, but he eventually reached a distant dressing station and afterwards made a splendid recovery.

It was a very narrow escape for Hame, inasmuch as only one other [of the party of eleven] is known to have survived.

Dr Fenwick, writing in the school magazine, March 1918

* Wiring – erecting wire entanglements

2nd Lieutenant W.W. Avins is knocked out by a 5.9 German shell – and then blown out of bed

2nd Lieutenant W.W. Avins was in action at Ypres on August 26th [1917] when he was knocked over by the concussion of a 5.9 shell. The hospital behind the lines [to which he was sent] was bombed by the enemy on November 12th, and Avins was literally blown out of bed. He has now been invalided home and appears to be making a very good recovery.

Dr Fenwick, writing in the school magazine, March 1918

A 'five nine' or 'five-point-nine' was a much-feared and highly destructive German high-explosive shell. It also referred to the gun that fired it.

H.B. Footner survives several battles but goes down with 'trench fever'

H.B. Footner, Pioneer, RE (Special Brigade), went out to France last March. He went 'up the line' in May, went into action at Messines and Ploegsteert, and was on the Ypres front from June to November, when he returned to England with trench fever. He has now recovered and rejoined.

Dr Fenwick, writing in the school magazine, March 1918

'TRENCH FEVER' AND 'TRENCH FOOT'

'Trench fever' was a somewhat undefined condition from which many troops suffered, including Pioneer Footner. It was a kind of rheumatic fever brought on by living for prolonged periods in the dreadfully cold, wet trenches, often for weeks at a time

'Trench foot' was frostbite in the feet and toes, again a common condition among those serving in trenches in the winter months. Incredibly, in the early part of the war, it was a crime to get trench foot – however, it was quickly realised that it was an inevitable consequence of trench warfare.

Lieutenant R.A. Wakely becomes a 'Boche Ammunition Carrier'

Lieut. R.A. Wakely, K.R.R. has been wounded with gunshot in the neck, and is in hospital in France.

He writes to us very cheerfully, and says he is quite fit, although he belongs to a 'stiff-necked and perverse generation' but hopes it will not be for long, as he is being operated on very shortly and hopes to be relieved of his duties as 'Boche Ammunition Carrier.'

We are pleased to hear – June 14th – that this operation was success-ful, and that Lieut. Wakely is nearly convalescent and is very shortly leaving the hospital.

Dr Fenwick, writing in the school magazine, July 1918

2nd Lieutenant D.L. Spickernell is wounded in ten places

D.L. Spickernell was sent on a daylight reconnaissance, but was unable to find the Boche, so had orders to advance his line. He then went on himself to reconnoitre in front, and suddenly came on a bombing block.

Mutually surprised, they forthwith began to attack each other. Spickernell got a Mills bomb amongst the Boches, but a stick bomb from them burst close to him, wounding him in ten places, one a bad one in the hip. This occurred on August 25th [1917] and he still has four pieces in him, otherwise he is getting on satisfactorily.

Dr Fenwick, writing in the school magazine, December, 1918

J.R. Miller has several bits of shrapnel removed from various parts of his body

I was wounded last August 23rd [1918]. We were just going 'over the top' when a 'Jerry' shell burst within a few yards of my gun team. Five of my men were killed and also my officer who was just behind me. The No. 2 and myself were wounded, but I hear that the No. 2 has since died.

When things cooled down a bit I crawled to the Aid Post, where my wounds were dressed. I was then able to get, with help, to the Advance Dressing Station, where I was put on a stretcher and taken to the CCS in a motor ambulance. I was kept here until late in the evening, when I was put on an ambulance train and taken to the 53rd General Hospital.

BOMBS AND SHRAPNEL

Mills Bomb: Named after its inventor, Sir William Mills (1865–1932), the Mills Bomb was the hand grenade adopted by the British Army in 1915. Serrated on the outside, it resembled a pineapple – hence its name (from the Spanish *granada*, pomegranate). It was designed to form shrapnel on explosion.

Stick Bomb: This was the German version of a hand grenade – cylindrical, with a rounded wooden handle and a string which had to be pulled sharply before the bomb was thrown.

Shrapnel: Named after General Henry Shrapnel (1761–1842), an officer in the Royal Artillery who invented a shell that came to be known as 'spherical case shot', consisting of a thin, fused, outer casing containing musket balls, and a charge that was enough to burst the casing in mid-flight and release the musket balls, which then careered onwards and outwards.

When he died in 1842, his family wanted to put up a monument to him, but could not afford to do so. Instead, they asked that the 'spherical case shot' should be renamed 'shrapnel shell'. As a result, their family name has the dubious distinction of being forever linked with mutilation and death.

Next morning I was X-rayed, and in the afternoon a piece of shrapnel was removed from my right thigh. I stayed at this hospital for a week, and then I was transferred to 'The Dublin' 83rd General Hospital for special treatment to the jaw.

After three days at this hospital they operated on my jaw, and also removed a piece of shrapnel from the left frontal area of my head. By this time, pieces of shrapnel which hit me in the left shoulder and back had worked to the surface and were picked out by one of the sisters.

Dr Fenwick, writing in the school magazine, December 1915

Lieutenant J.G Jones is wounded a second time, and then gassed

Lieut. J.G.C. Jones has been wounded a second time, having been hit just below the knee. We understand that, early in one of the 'big' movements on the Western Front, Jones was sent to the rear suffering from gas poisoning. On the way he was physically sick, and felt so much better afterwards that he decided to return to the firing line.

This he very pluckily did, only to be knocked out by a severe wound in the leg. For this he did not get proper treatment at the time, and it became 'touch-and-go' as to whether he would lose his leg.

We are glad to say that amputation was found to be unnecessary, and that Jones is now at home in a state of convalescence.

Dr Fenwick, writing in the school magazine, December 1915

2nd Lieutenant J.T. Snelgar – 'a Hun bullet pinked me'

The luck that has been with me for over a year in the trenches did not desert me in this last scrap, for it was not until July 5th in the Leipsic Redoubt that a Hun bullet pinked me and made it very uncomfortable for me to sit down for some days.

However, I could walk about and the scarcity of officers made it imperative for me to carry on. On the 7th we made another attack in the morning and the Huns strafed us all day with heavy shrapnel to get their own back, but our fellows held on despite heavy casualties until they were relieved at night.

The school magazine, July 1916

1 Dr Edward Fenwick ('Tig'), first headmaster of Bournemouth School, 1901–32. Dr Fenwick remains something of an enigma, for there are virtually no remaining documents by him or about him in the present school. Even his memorial tablet in Bournemouth Crematorium gives no indication of his dates, though we do know that he died in the summer of 1940, just before the Battle of Britain. He would, most certainly, have been just as proud of the Old Boys in the Second World War, as he was of his own ex-pupils in the Great War.

2 Bournemouth School when it opened in 1901. This school was built on open land on the outskirts of Bournemouth. Thomas Hardy had written in his *Tess of the d'Urbevilles*, published just ten years earlier in 1891, that 'not a sod had been turned there since the days of the Caesars'. The school moved to new premises in another outlying part of Bournemouth in September 1939, coinciding exactly with the outbreak of the Second World War. Sadly, many of the old records of the school may have been lost in that move.

Opposite 4 Fourteen 'Distinguished Candidates' in 1907. Dr Fenwick's examination results were phenomenal – he must have been a hugely inspirational teacher. All these pupils had gained various honours and distinctions. Tragically, two of them were to be killed in the Great War: P.J. Johnson, standing fifth from the left, and J.R. Turner, seated last on the right. G.H. Mate, standing first on the left, served as Vice Consul in Syria during the war, and his letters appear in this book. P.J. Grigg (later Sir James Grigg) standing third from the left, gained a special Cambridge prize for being first of all Senior Boys throughout the country.

3 Dr Fenwick with the first intake of fifty-four boys and just four assistant masters. Many of these boys grew up to fight in the 'Great War' of 1914-18, which was to break out just as they were starting their careers. Five of the boys in this photograph were killed: W.P. Baker, H.W. Froud, F.O. Hodges, W.E. Okey and R.F. Purkess, but today there is no way of identifying them in this photo.

5 Dr Fenwick with three of his most brilliant pupils: C.A. Kershaw, N. Wragg and D.C. Colborne. The three pupils here achieved outstanding results in the Cambridge Senior Local Examinations. Kershaw had come first of 3,196 candidates in December 1915. Wragg had come first of 2,777 candidates in December 1913 and also first of 2,846 candidates in December 1914. Colborne had come first of 2,419 candidates in December 1915. All three survived the Great War, and Norman Wragg gained a Military Cross.

6 William A.R. Alder, 1900–17.

Pioneer, Royal Engineers Signal Service.

Killed in action, 30 July 1917. Aged 17.

Of all the sacrifices which the war has made
so painfully familiar to us, surely none is more
piteous than this – the spilling of the life-
blood of a boy scarcely more than a child of
seventeen years.
   Dr Fenwick, the school magazine, December 1917

7 Jesse Marson Atkin, BA, 1891–1914,
Assistant Master

Lieutenant, 3rd Battalion, Sherwood Foresters

Killed in action at Ploegstreet, 7 November
1914. Aged 23.

Mr Atkin's influence was chiefly felt in the
deep personal interest he took in his boys,
every one of whom regarded him – and with
good reason – as a friend.
   Dr Fenwick, the school magazine, December 1914

8 2nd Lieutenant Hubert Dinwoodie, MC.

Awarded the Military Cross for 'conspicuous gallantry'.

During an attack by the enemy, although his gun emplacement was destroyed by a shell and the gun partially buried, he immediately got it into action again, and, after firing till his ammunition was exhausted, removed the gun into safety. He then, though partially incapacitated, led parties with ammunition and bombs up to the firing line.

Citation, 31 May 1916

9 2nd Lieutenant (Temporary Captain) R. Drayton, MC.

Awarded the Military Cross for 'conspicuous gallantry'.

When, after a heavy bombardment, the enemy raided our trenches, although wounded, he collected a few men and repulsed all attacks on a portion of the trench. He set a fine example to all around him.

Citation, 26 June 1916

10 Francis Forman, 1888–1916. Assistant Master.

2nd Lieutenant, Dorset Regiment.

Killed in action, 14 July 1916. Aged 28.

In Mr Forman we not only lost a highly valued member of the staff, but one who endeared himself by his courteous and obliging disposition to all – masters and boys alike – with whom he came into contact.

Dr Fenwick, the school magazine, July 1916

11 Harold W. Froud, 1889–1917.

2nd Lieutenant, Durham Light Infantry.

Died of wounds, 27 July 1917. Aged 28.

Froud entered the School a very short time after the day it was opened, and when there were less than sixty boys on the register... He was a boy of extraordinarily fine character, with a great charm of manner. A good all-round sportsman, he shone particularly as an athlete. He was our Senior 'Champion' in 1906.

Dr Fenwick, the school magazine, December 1917

12 Frank E. Game, 1896–1918.

Private, South Staffordshire Infantry.

Died from shell–gas poisoning, 7 June 1918. Aged 21.

Of the many hundreds of boys who have passed through our gates, not one could claim to be more completely a product of the School than 'Freddy' Game, and there are few indeed whose names have been recorded so frequently and so deservedly on our 'honours' boards. The annual examination records of a complete decade, covering the whole of his School life and one year as an 'Old Boy' include, with an unbroken sequence, the name of F.E. Game as achieving distinguished success in one form or another.

Dr Fenwick, the school magazine, July 1918

13 Claude Graham, 1892–1916.

Hampshire Regiment.

Died of malaria at Alexandria, 13 November 1916. Aged 23.

Graham came to us from the North-Eastern County School, Barnard Castle... He passed the Cambridge Junior Local Examination just before he left, and then he took up 'Pharmacy' with his father... He was a most exemplary son and a general favourite.

Dr Fenwick, the school magazine, December 1916

14 William H. Gunning, 1893–1916.

2nd Lieutenant, Hampshire Regiment.

Died of wounds, 31 October 1916. Aged 23.

W.H. Gunning was the younger of two
brothers who were educated partly here and
partly at Bristol Grammar School. During
the latter part of his stay here he was a
member of the OTC, and he shewed both
keenness and efficiency.

Dr Fenwick, the school magazine, December 1916

15 Douglas G. Hazard, 1894–1915.

2nd Lieutenant, 2nd Shropshire
Light Infantry.

Reported missing, believed killed, 25 May 1915.
Aged 21.

Hazard was a boy of whom the School had
good reason to be proud. His record was in
every way honourable, his character was of
the best, and he had the magnetic power of
making friends wherever he went. He was
one of the earliest to enlist after the war
broke out.

Dr Fenwick, the school magazine, March 1916

16 Charles S. Martin, 1890–1917.

2nd Lieutenant, 6th Battalion,
Leicester Regiment.

Killed in action, 4 October 1917. Aged 26.

Of the three brothers Martin who were educated
here, Charlie was the second. Always very keen
on sport, he was one of the best cricketers we ever
had. Against Southampton Grammar School,
by making a score of fifty-four and taking four
wickets at but a small cost, he had the lion's share
in bringing victory to our side in 1907.

Dr Fenwick, the school magazine, December 1917

17 Brian B. New, 1891–1917.

2nd Lieutenant, Duke of Cornwall's
Light Infantry.

Killed in action, 16 August 1917. Aged 26.

No one of those who were privileged to know
a 'Barry' New could fail to think of him with
affection and esteem. He was essentially a boy
of the right type, he could always be depended
upon to do his best, and his influence was always
for good. He was a Prefect, a member of the
OTC (in which he reached the rank of Colonel
Sergeant) for six years, Captain of the Cricket
XI, a prominent member of the Football XI, and
before leaving he attained to the Sixth Form and
passed the Cambridge Senior Local.

Dr Fenwick, the school magazine, December 1917

18 'Little Willie' was the name jeeringly given to one of the early prototypes of 'tanks', designed from July 1915 as a war engine specifically to cross a 5ft trench. The name refers to the Kaiser's son, Crown Prince Wilhelm. It wasn't very successful, with its ungainly rear steering wheels – but at least it paved the way to later, more successful models. This survivor can be seen at Bovington Tank Museum in Dorset.

19 The Thiépval Memorial is a gigantic structure of red brick, faced with Portland stone, commemorating 72,000 British and Commonwealth soldiers who died in the Battle of the Somme, but who have no known grave. Their names are carved on the sixteen piers at its base. It was designed by Edward Lutyens, who had previously designed the Cenotaph in Whitehall, London, and it was unveiled on 31 July 1932 by the then Prince of Wales (later to become King Edward VIII and subsequently the Duke of Windsor). It is 150ft (46m) high, with foundations 19ft (6m) thick. Four former pupils from Bournemouth School are recorded here: W.P. Baker, C.E. Harbord, W.O. Cooper and S.H. Thrift.

Above left 20 The Military Cross (MC): this award was created in 1914 for 'gallantry during active operations against the enemy'. It was awarded to commissioned officers of the substantive rank of Captain or below and for Warrant Officers. It is a silver cross with straight arms, with the Royal Cypher in the centre. The reverse is plain but engraved with the recipient's name. The ribbon is blue and white. One master and seventeen former pupils of Bournemouth School won the MC, with A.H. Baker gaining an MC and Bar. The MC shown here was won in Mesopotamia by the Revd M. Roy Smith, a Methodist Minister and grandfather of a former Bournemouth School pupil.

Above right 21 'Your Country Needs You'. Lord Kitchener's fiercely commanding poster urged Tig's Boys and the whole of that generation to volunteer for military service. Kitchener was in charge of recruiting those hundreds of thousands of young men who were needed to fight – and their resulting enthusiasm to join up was overwhelming. Several versions of this poster were produced at intervals as the war continued. (Imperial War Museum, PST 2735)

Opposite 23 'Dulce et Decorum est.' Wilfred Owen's memorable poem about the horrors of being gassed is the final answer to those who thought it 'sweet and noble' to die fighting for one's country. This line of blinded soldiers helps us to sympathise with Frank Ernest Game, one of Tig's Boys, a former Bournemouth School pupil who was killed by poisonous gas in June 1918, aged just twenty-one. (Imperial War Museum, Q 11586)

22 'The chief trouble… is the awfully boggy ground.' It's hard to visualise just how filthy and boggy the ground had become after months of warfare. This picture shows a tank abandoned in the muddy squalor. Read the account of A.H. Baker on p. 39 as he describes how he rescued a tank in such conditions. Serving in the Tank Salvage Company, he won an MC and Bar for his skill and courage. (Imperial War Museum, CO2241)

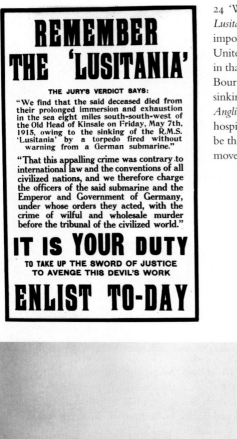

24 'Wilful and wholesale murder.' The sinking of RMS *Lusitania* by a German submarine was an event of great importance. It shocked the world – in particular the United States, as 124 innocent US citizens lost their lives in that unprovoked attack. One wounded ex-pupil from Bournemouth School, Maurice Hellier, witnessed the sinking of the *Lusitania* together with another ship, the *Anglia*, as he was being brought back to England in the hospital ship *Newhaven*. He thought his own ship would be the next attacked – but luckily for him, the submarine moved away. See p. 88. (Imperial War Museum, Q33149)

25 The sinking of the battlecruiser HMS *Queen Mary*. The Battle of Jutland took place on 31 May 1916 (see p.150). This dramatic but somewhat obscure photograph shows the tremendous explosion as the English battlecruiser HMS *Queen Mary* was hit twice by the German battlecruiser *Derfflinger*, and blew up, killing and drowning 1,266 members of her crew – among whom was the twenty-year-old ex-Bournemouth School pupil, Hermann Meyer. Only eighteen of the crew survived. The wreck of the HMS *Queen Mary* was discovered in 1991, and found to be resting partly upside down on sand 197ft (60m) deep. (Imperial War Museum, SP1708)

26 '…A lot of long marching to do…' A typical scene as a line of men march along nondescript terrain in the dusk. Read Arthur Wolfe's letter on p. 24–25 for a description of marching 'from one point of the line to another, which carrying a heavy pack on your back, tires one out more than anything else'. He was killed in action just one week after writing that letter, at Neuve Chapelle. (Imperial War Museum, Q3014)

27 'Well, if you knows of a better 'ole, go to it.' In his letter describing the trenches (see p.43–44) Maurice Hellier describes the complicated maze of lines and 'saps' on the Western Front. In fact any and every 'hole' which could afford protection was a welcome shelter, whether it was a bomb crater or a tree-stump. The men in this photograph were lucky to have found some really superior 'funk-holes' – much better than Old Bill's boggy shell-crater drawn by Bruce Bairnsfather, shown on the following page.

"Well, if you knows of a better 'ole, go to it."

Left 28 Here is the original famous cartoon by Bruce Bairnsfather (1888–1959), showing a pair of soldiers stuck in a shell-hole. Bairnsfather was an extremely popular cartoonist of the war, remembered particularly for his characters of 'Old Bill' – a grumpy, walrus-moustached old soldier – and 'Little Alphie', his youngest troopmate. The caption became so famous that in 1917 *The Better 'Ole* was actually staged as a musical in London and on Broadway, and two silent films were made with that title. (© 2011 Barbara Bruce Bairnsfather. All Rights Reserved.)

Right 29 Another cartoon by Bairnsfather, gently mocking the military world of red tape and absurd requests. It gives a good impression of the chaos as experienced by the ordinary 'Tommy'. (© 2011 Barbara Bruce Bairnsfather. All Rights Reserved.)

"There goes our blinkin' parapet again."

The Things that Matter.

Scene : Loos, during the September offensive.
Colonel Fitz-Shrapnel receives the following message from "G.H.Q.":—
"Please let us know, as soon as possible, the number of tins of raspberry jam issued to you last Friday."

Left 30 Yet another of Bairnsfather's vast number of cartoons – this one depicting the stolid fatalism of a typical soldier – who looks out quite dispassionately at the appalling scene outside, regarding it simply as a petty nuisance he has to put up with. These cartoons were great morale-boosters. (© 2011 Barbara Bruce Bairnsfather. All Rights Reserved.)

Lieutenant E.F. Gunning is 'blinded for some days through shock'

Lieut. E.F. Gunning, London Regiment, was wounded on July 15th [1916]. He lay unconscious for 20 hours, and was blind for some days through shock. Writing on July 29th he says: 'My wound was not of a serious nature as I am already out of hospital and convalescent.'

The school magazine, December 1916

Three months later, E.F. Gunning's brother, William Herbert Gunning, died of wounds, aged 23, buried in Malta.

2nd Lieutenant J.T. Snelgar – 'My luck was extraordinary' (but he still gets a shell fragment in his thigh)

My luck was extraordinary. During the morning three fellows were hit while talking to me, and my helmet was several times struck by heavy pieces of shell and knocked quite out of shape.

Yet it was not until the afternoon that a high explosive shell 30 yards away sent a small fragment into my thigh and compelled me to retire to my dug-out out of the rain and mud. As company commander I had had a pretty strenuous time for five or six days, and the rest in hospital was most welcome.

There one heard from all sides that the Germans invariably lost in hand to hand fighting – in the case of the Wilts' attack on the 7th, Fritz was out and over his parados [earthworks] before our fellows reached his trench.

Prisoners caught in dug-outs confirmed one another in stating they realised their fight to be a losing one. But the task before the British is tremendous, as Verdun has proved, and if we succeed in breaking the line the end will be in sight, otherwise a slow and battering form of advance will be necessary to compel the Huns to accept our terms.

The school magazine, July 1916

'OVER THE TOP'

Reginald Fairley goes 'over the top', is wounded in the throat and jaw, and 'then came blackness'

We received orders from the trench headquarters that we were to make a charge as soon as we got into position, which was before 5.30 a.m., as we were to go 'over the top' at that time. Owing to our imperfect knowledge of these trenches we were not near our position till 8 a.m. In the meantime we halted for breakfast.

Then came the order to 'Off packs and leave 'em in the trench; load rifles and fix bayonets.' We were to proceed to our position and be ready to charge at 9.30 a.m., after ten minutes bombarding by the artillery. We started off, and soon came across evidences of the earlier fighting. We had to pass under the German barbed wire by means of a trench which had been dug a few days before. Our troops were holding the second line of German trenches. The poor beggars had been in over 48 hours, and their water-bottles had given out, and as they were terribly thirsty we gave them a pull from our bottles.

We were now told to get into a sort of ditch, about 4ft deep, in front of the trench they were holding, and charge from that. We were to go straight ahead for about 20 yards, then wheel to the left, and clear the Germans off the top of a large heap of slag.

We had to go in a crouching attitude to get into the ditch. An old Boer War man led the way, I was second. We were to make our way up the trench till our company was all in. That ditch was a sight: blood everywhere, great clots and splashes on the sides, and pools of it in the bottom.

At last we were ready, crouched, waiting for the word; and how my heart beat.

I peeped up to get a look at the ground in front, but a bullet kicked up the earth close to my face, so I got down again. At last a shout sounded from the right which acted like an electric shock. With one bound we were over the bank and racing across the open, yelling like only Kentish men can.

The air was filled with a whistling sound, and the crackle of rifle and machine guns showed that the Germans were ready for us. Some of them ran out of their trenches, and started bolting to get behind the slag heap. I dropped on one knee and bowled one over. Our fellows were falling in all directions. A couple of seconds later I dropped again, and potted another German. Lots of our fellows were doing the same.

Then we went for the slag heap. Up the steep ascent we went cheering like mad. The Germans didn't wait for us, but got down on the opposite side into a trench, where they waited for us with machine guns and bombs and grenades. We rushed across to the edge of the coal, and had to drop and take cover, for the Germans poured a heavy volley into us as soon as we appeared on the edge.

I fired my rifle into the thick of them, and had the satisfaction of seeing one drop, so I told the fellow on my right as we lay on the coal. He said: 'I must have a pot at them.'

'For God's sake be careful how you look over,' I said, 'as they are waiting for us.' Up he got on his knees, gave a little sob, and pitched over backwards into a shell crater behind him. I peeped into the crater to see what was wrong with him. He lay head downwards. I never felt upset; I guess I was too excited. I now found time to look round me. Out of 200 men only about 30 had succeeded in reaching the slag heap, and some of them were wounded.

I had a bullet hole through my pocket, and the strap of my haversack was shot away. We lay waiting for some of our bombers to come up and bomb the Germans out of the trenches in front of us. Only one officer was left with us. He crawled away to the right to see if there was any chance of us doing anything; I never saw him again. I expect he was killed.

We then noticed a German peeping over the coal 30 yards away. The fellow on my left said to me, 'You shoot, and I'll see what effect it has.' So I waited, with my rifle trained on the spot. Up came his head again. I sighted carefully and pressed the trigger. His head gave a little jerk. 'Good shot,' said my companion, 'you got him dead between the eyes.' I felt quite delighted.

Then I got another fellow farther away on the left. One of our bombers managed to reach us. He started lobbing bombs over the edge. We heard them burst, followed by shrieks and groans.

It was then I got my first wound. A rifle bullet from a German sniper passed through my left hand and came out at the base of the thumb. The man near me sang out, 'I'm hit.' The back of his hand was torn across by a piece of shell. We crawled into a crater and bound each other's wounds up with our field dressing.

While we were there another fellow crawled into the crater. 'Good heavens,' he said, 'isn't this awful. I believe we three are the only ones able to move. What shall we do?' So we held a confab. We agreed that the best plan would be to leave the slag heap and bolt for the trench that we had seen the Germans run out of. We got off the heap all right, and made a dash for the trench. Immediately we heard the rifles crack, and I felt a stinging pain in my left thigh, and knew I was hit. I thought I would drop and take cover.

Before I could do so I felt the shock of a bullet in my right arm; that caused me to drop my rifle. At the same instant two bullets struck me in the left shoulder, and as I flung myself to the ground a bullet coming from the right flank entered my throat just under my chin and exploded.

My head went up with a jerk, and I felt the jaw-bones smash; then came blackness.

The school magazine, December 1916

A HAPPY SEQUEL TO THE PREVIOUS ACCOUNT

A lucky few of the wounded prisoners of war are sent to Switzerland, where they are given a huge welcome, and treated as heroes

REGINALD FAIRLEY DESCRIBES HIS ARRIVAL THERE

... We were then handed over to a Swiss officer and some Swiss soldiers. At last the train moved off, and in five minutes we were across the border.

The embankment was lined with people, who cheered and showered flowers upon us. It was five minutes off 8 p.m. when we crossed the border, and at 8 o'clock we stopped at the first little station in Switzerland.

All the inhabitants were at the station to see us and give us presents of tobacco, cigarettes, chocolate and huge bunches of flowers, Union Jacks and Swiss flags were flying everywhere. A lady told us that it would be the same thing all along the line, and the more so when we got to our destination. Our first stop was Berne: the station was simply packed with people.

We could not take the things in fast enough. Huge wreaths of flowers, Swiss and British flags, packets of chocolate and cigarettes, pipes, and tobacco, biscuits, cakes of scented soap, packets of stationery, patent cigarette lighters, combs, razers, folding scissors, huge bunches of roses and lilies tied with red, white and blue ribbons.

The carriages were one mass of flowers, and tied on the bunches were cards with 'Welcome glorious soldiers of England,' and 'May your noble country be victorious,' and 'God speed you brave soldiers,' and similar inscriptions. We only stopped about five minutes at Berne.

We reached Lucerne at 1. a.m., and despite the lateness or rather the earliness of the hour, the station was full. We left the train and were marched into the big refreshment room, through a lance of cheering people. There we were served with coffee, bread and butter, cakes, etc. Huge Union Jacks were hung everywhere and we could not cope with the masses of flowers and presents which were thrust upon us.

We left Lucerne at 3 a.m. and arrived at Montreux about 6 a.m. The people of this place were even more enthusiastic than the other places. We marched out of the station to the tune of 'Tipperary,' with a full brass band, to the largest hotel in the place, the Hotel Suisse.

The entrance hall was lined on either side with crowds of little girls, dressed in white with little black jackets and big black hats, who cheered us vociferously. Out on the roof garden large tables were laid out for breakfast, and hosts of ladies took charge of us. The hotel was hung with flags all over.

After breakfast an old gentleman got up and made speeches to the crowd, finishing up by asking for three cheers for the most noble, the most gallant and heroic British Army, and they were given with a will. The band struck up our National Anthem, the Marseillaise, and the Swiss National Anthem; more cheering. We split up in groups and related our experiences to the ladies and answered their many questions.

We took our departure to the railway station, the band playing the same tune as before. We are now on the last stage of our journey. All up over the hill-tops in an electric train, along the edge of precipices, and through lengthy tunnels till at last we reached Chateaux d'Oex.

Here, another reception was prepared for us, and more refreshments. The whole village was decorated with flags, and as we came from the station, people from the windows of their houses showered flowers upon us.

It seems as if all my troubles were over. The valley is perfectly beautiful, surrounded by snow-clad peaks and wooded hills. The hotel at which we were quartered is very nice. Each bed has nice clean sheets, spring mattresses and feather pillows, so different from the prison camp.

The night of our arrival a thanksgiving service was held in the Protestant Church. It is next door to the hotel, so we did not have far to go. The church was decorated with flowers and ferns. Large Swiss and British flags hung over the chancel steps, and two Union Jacks were crossed above the altar. The air here is simply wonderful; I feel the benefit of it already. We turn in at 10 p.m., and I can assure you we sleep like tops.

The school magazine, December 1916

2nd Lieutenant Arnold Whitting is lucky to get a 'Blighty'

My wound is not at all serious, and I think I am exceedingly lucky to be back in England again so soon. A fragment of the bomb caught me in the upper part of the calf and went clean through, coming out a little lower down, thus making two holes, about 4 or 5 inches apart.

It has not been very painful, but was just bad enough to get me back to 'Blighty.' I had to have a slight operation to prevent blood-poisoning, but, as they gave me an anaesthetic, I knew nothing about it.

The school magazine, December 1915

Captain M.J. Hellier is wounded twice and then taken prisoner

Captain M.J. Hellier, previously reported missing March 22nd [1918] is now reported prisoner of war in Germany.

Captain Hellier has served in the Army since the beginning of the war. He went to France in the spring of 1915, and was in action within a month of his arrival. In November of the same year he was wounded in both arms and was in hospital for some months.

After again being passed fit for duty he rejoined his battalion in France and was in the Somme battle of 1916. In August of that year he was wounded and suffered from shell concussion, but did not leave France, and within a short time was back in the fighting line.

Of the original officers who went out with his battalion in 1915, only three remained who went into action with him at dawn on March 21st. The Colonel, who was one, was killed, and in the evening of March 22nd, after they had been heavily attacked twice within the hour, Captain Hellier, who, with his company, occupied an isolated position, was surrounded in the thick mist and darkness and captured.

Dr Fenwick, writing in the school magazine, July 1918

Five

TIG TELLS OF NINETY-EIGHT DEATHS

Obituaries of former pupils appeared regularly in the school magazine from December 1914 to December 1918 and even beyond – well after the war had ended. They were obviously written by Dr Fenwick himself. He knew them all – little boys growing into big boys, then leaving school to be slaughtered. Some had been boarders and were personally looked after by 'Tig' and his wife, so they were virtually part of his own family.

Here, in Tig's own words, are accounts of how these boys died, taken from the school magazine. It's particularly poignant to note that the first of these former pupils of the school, William Alder, was only 17 when he was killed.

MASTERS

Jesse Marson Atkin

Killed in action, 7 November 1914. Aged 23.
Lieutenant, 3rd Battalion, Sherwood Foresters.
Ploegsteert Memorial, Comines-Warneton, Hainaut, Belgium. Panel 7.

Mr Atkin became an assistant master here in January 1913, and very soon gained the high esteem of masters and boys for the keen and active interest he took in all that concerned the welfare of the school.

He took a commission in the Special Reserve of Officers soon after he came to us, being gazetted to the Sherwood Foresters, and when the war broke out he gladly responded to the call for help.

For the first three months he did garrison duty at Plymouth, and it was not until the end of October that he got the chance he was longing for, to join the British Forces in France. One letter, received after he had reached the fighting zone, showed that he was in the best of health and spirits, and it came as a great shock to us all to read his name in the list of killed published in the newspapers of November 24th.

The school magazine, December 1914

The manner in which Mr Akin was killed is typical of the fate of millions. It is worth printing the letter written by the Colonel commanding the 3rd Worcesters, the regiment to which Lieutenant Atkin was attached. It is also worth noting that although he was a master, he was aged only 23 – and must have only just left college when he came to teach at Bournemouth School.

On the morning of 7th November [1914], the Germans attacked and rushed one of our trenches east of Ploegsteert Wood. Two of our Companies (B and D, the latter to which Lieutenant Atkin belonged), were in reserve in the wood. They both were launched in a counter-attack, and as they neared the edge of the wood were subjected to a very heavy fire. Lieutenant Atkin, who had just turned his head to give some directions, was shot in the back of the neck, and practically expired at once. He just said "Goodbye" to the man nearest him, who had run to his assistance.

The wood was very thick with undergrowth, and the platoon Lieutenant Atkin was with was slowly moved round farther to the left. At dark, our Battalion was relieved by some of the Lancashire Fusiliers and Argyll and Sutherland Highlanders. Prior to this, search parties had been sent out by both B and D Companies to collect all who had been killed or wounded. In the dark and thick wood only a certain number were found that evening, and I regret to say the Lieutenant Atkin was not among them. Some days later the Somersetshire Light Infantry reported that they had found a subaltern belonging to the regiment near the edge of the wood and had buried him there. As Lieutenant Atkin was the only subaltern killed in that neighbourhood, they have concluded that the officer buried by the Somerset Light Infantry was Lieutenant Atkin.

Francis Forman

Killed in action, 14 July 1916. Aged 28.
2nd Lieutenant, 3rd Battalion, Dorset Regiment.
Thiépval Memorial, Somme, France. Pier and Face 7. B

He was appointed an assistant master at this School on April 26th, 1909. He left us, temporarily we hoped, to take a commission in the 3rd Battalion, Dorset Regiment, at the end of the summer term, 1915, and after a period of training at Wyke Regis he left for the seat of war of France on June 29th, being attached to the 1/7th Royal Warwickshire Regiment.

A telegram from the War Office announced that he was killed on July 14th.

The school magazine, July 1916

Percy David Foley Dean

Killed in action, 26 June 1916. Aged 29.
Pioneer, Royal Engineers, Special Brigade (Chemists).
Sucrerie Military Cemetery, Colincamps, Somme, France. I. F. 19.

He came to us as an assistant master in September, 1915, to fill a 'war' vacancy, and left at the end of that term, having obtained admission as a pioneer to a Special Brigade (Chemists) of the Royal Engineers.

The school magazine, July 1916

Harry Tiplady

Died, 17 September 1914. Aged 26.
2nd Lieutenant in the School OTC.
Tiplady died at his home in Darlington.

Mr Tiplady joined the staff of this School in September, 1911, and very soon established for himself a reputation as a teacher of the very highest class. During the three years he was with us the results gained in examinations by his pupils were absolutely phenomenal. His special subject was Science, but anything he undertook to do was well done.

He was 2nd Lieutenant in the OTC and the work he did there was particularly valuable, more especially with regard to signalling and shooting.

Mr Tiplady had a severe attack of appendicitis on Saturday, September 12th, at his home in Darlington. An operation was performed the following day, but he did not rally and the end came on Thursday, September 19th.

The school magazine, December 1914

TIG'S BOYS
Ex-Pupils of Bournemouth School

William Arthur Redvers Alder

Killed in action, 30 July, 1917. Aged 17.
Pioneer, RE Signal Service.
Potijze Chateau Lawn Cemetery, Ypres, West-Vlaanderen, Belgium.
A. 20.

Of all the sacrifices which the war has made so painfully familiar to us, surely none is more piteous than this – the spilling of the life-blood of a boy, scarcely more than a child, of 17 years.

Alder left us before he had reached an age to take a leading part in school affairs, but he will long be remembered as a quiet, well-meaning boy, who never gave trouble and who could be depended upon to do to the best of his ability whatever duty fell to his lot.

He joined our OTC in September, 1914, and remained a member till he left the school.

Enlisting in the Royal Engineers, he was put into the Signal Service (Wireless Section) and sent to France last July. On the 28th he was posted for duty with his section and ordered with three others to proceed to a forward test point of some importance. The journey was done partly by motor lorry, and partly on foot.

In the latter stage the party being heavily laden with equipment, some boxes and bags of rations were left by the road side. The distance to the new dug-out was not great, and, as all was quiet on arrival, the Sergeant sent back a small squad (of whom Alder was one) to retrieve the rations which had been dumped.

Less than five minutes afterwards, a shell burst very near them, and Alder was badly hit. Stretcher bearers were speedily summoned and he was at once carried off and well cared for, but he lingered only a few hours.

The school magazine, December 1917

Bernard Charles Jeeves Allbon

Died in hospital, 3 February 1919. Aged 22.
Captain, 3rd Battalion, Dorset Regiment.
Wimborne Road Cemetery, Bournemouth. O. 5. 110. S.

... he was in the thick of the terrible fighting which took place during the German onslaught of last Spring [1918] and he came through it with a high degree of credit. The large number of casualties amongst his brother officers compelled him to assume command of his unit and he brought it back to safety under what must have been truly appalling conditions.

Some indication of the stress under which he laboured at this time may be gathered from the fact that for 37 hours in succession he had no food and for a period of 18 days he was never able to take off his clothes for a night's sleep.

At Neuvilly, on October 10, whilst giving his last orders preparatory to leading his men into battle, he received a severe wound in the leg, which necessitated his removal – first to the Base and then to a Red Cross Hospital at Brighton. Three operations were performed on him there, quite successfully, but after the third he was attacked by the most virulent form of influenza, and he succumbed, on February 3, 1919, to heart failure.

His body was brought to Bournemouth and buried, with full military honours, at the Wimborne Road Cemetery [in Bournemouth], Dr Fenwick and the officers of our OTC being present.

The school magazine, April 1919

Edgar Philip Ayling

Missing and assumed killed, 25 March 1918. Aged 25.
A.B. 'A' Company, Drake Battalion, RND.
Arras Memorial, Pas de Calais, France. Bay 1.

Ayling... went through the greater part of the Gallipoli campaign. Returning to England he was sent to France (though not properly recovered from the effects of dysentery)... drafted in the 'Drake' Battalion which – within a week – was engaged in the disastrous fighting of the end of March, 1918. He was reported missing (now assumed killed) near High Wood, Gouzean Court, France.

The school magazine, December 1919

Edgar Ayling was a cousin of another Old Boy of Bournemouth School, Frederick John White, killed in action on 8 June 1918.

Walter George William Bailey

Killed, 15 September 1916. Aged 20.
Captain, 15th Battalion, Hampshire Regiment.
Serre Road Cemetery No. 2, Somme, France. XXXVIII. A. 10.

... After leaving school he went to Queens' College, Cambridge, where he was a member of the University OTC. In the following June he obtained a transfer to a newly formed Hampshire battalion and was quickly promoted Lieutenant and then Captain. He went to France in April, 1916, and soon obtained the command of his company. He was killed at the commencement of the attack on Flers.

His Colonel wrote: – 'He died leading his men to a very substantial victory and that poor consolation I offer as no man could do more. He was beloved by everyone and he was the smartest officer I have ever seen for his service. He is a loss to the profession he intended to embrace and had he lived he must have risen to rank far above that of a company commander.'

The school magazine, December 1916

Wilfred James Bailey

Killed in action, 2 December 1917. Aged 29.
Private, Inniskilling Fusiliers.
Cambrai Memorial, Louverval, Nord, France. Panels 5 and 6.

October, 1914, found him in 'khaki' as a Sergeant in the Army Pay Corps. Two and a half years later he was drafted into the Staffordshire Regiment, reverting to private's rank, but retaining sergeant's pay and allowances. Ordered to France on August 16th, 1917, he was transferred on arrival to the Inniskilling Fusiliers, so that he had but little more than three months' active service on the Western Front before he was killed. His death was instantaneous.

Bailey was married in May, 1917, and leaves a widow to mourn his loss.

The school magazine, March 1918

Walter Percy Baker

Killed in action, 14 July 1916. Aged 28.
2nd Lieutenant, Dorset Regiment.
Thiépval Memorial, Somme, France. Pier and Face 9 A, 9 B and 10 B.

W.P. Baker was one of the 'original' members of the School; in fact his name appears first of those who applied for admission nearly 16 years ago... He volunteered immediately on the outbreak of war, and joined the Hants Cyclists Regiment, receiving his commission some months later. He went to the front with his regiment on June 27th – only 17 days before his death...

According to Lieut. Oxberry [who had written to tell of Baker's death], it seems that Lieut. Baker met his death whilst gallantly attempting to carry into safety a wounded sergeant of his regiment... 'Percy was with his platoon in the attack and his sergeant told me all about it. They worked a machine-gun as long as they could, and then had to leave that portion of the trench, and that is where Percy endeavoured to carry one of the platoon sergeants who was hit. He was carrying him when he was slightly hit. Sergeant Woodley then took the wounded sergeant from Percy, who then just raised his head above the parapet, and was again hit.

The school magazine, December 1916

THE ARRIVAL OF TANKS ON THE BATTLEFIELD:
LITTLE WILLIES AND BIG WILLIES

The successful Battle of Flers, at which Walter Bailey was killed *(see page 111)*, is historically important because the village of Flers, north-west of Alençon, was where tanks were first used in battle.

This weird contraption was promptly nicknamed 'Little Willie', after the German Imperial Crown Prince Wilhelm. Later, a larger version of it was called 'Big Willie', after his father, Emperor Wilhelm II of Germany – The Kaiser.

Tanks were a British invention, kept as a closely-guarded secret and intended to strike terror into the German ranks, offering an impregnably safe vehicle for attack. Sadly for these early versions, they were incredibly unreliable, with poor vision and navigation. They moved at a snail's pace – half a mile per hour.

At Flers, the British tried to deploy all the tanks they possessed – forty-nine in all. However, of these, seventeen failed even to reach the frontline. Of the remaining twenty-two, seven failed to start when given the signal to attack – so just fifteen managed to rumble forward into no man's land. Nevertheless, the Germans troops were utterly demoralised – at least on this first encounter.

Bernard Frampton Barnes

Killed in action, 18 September 1918. Aged 22.
2/24th London Regiment.
Vis-en-Artois Memorial, Pas de Calais, France. Panel 10.

He went first to France (in June, 1916), and – at the end of the year – to Salonika. There he was trained as a Signaller, a branch of the service in which he took much interest, and he was attached to Company HQ.

After six months on this front he was drafted to Palestine, and, with his regiment, he was among the first to enter the captured city of Jerusalem. Passing straight through, they met and drove off the Turks on the further side.

In July, after a year in Palestine, the Regiment was brought back again to France, and a month afterwards he had a well-earned and most thoroughly enjoyed 'leave' of 14 days at home.

Soon after his return he fell in action at Peizière, France, after three years of service for his country. No details are to hand except the fact that his body was found, in the neighbourhood of Company HQ, and in circumstances which indicated that he had been killed instantaneously.

The school magazine, April 1919

Norman Barrow

Went down with HMS *Hampshire*, 5 June 1916. Aged 22
Engine Room Artificer, HMS *Hampshire*.
Portsmouth Naval Memorial, *Hampshire*, 15.

He was a member of the engine room staff of HMS *Hampshire*, which took part in the naval battle of Jutland [31 May 1916], and which so soon afterwards sank with practically all hands off the north coast of Scotland. Lord Kitchener and his staff were amongst those who went down in the ill-fated ship.

The school magazine, July 1916

Laurie Bell

Accidentally killed, 29 July 1918. Aged 19.
2nd Lieutenant, RAF.
Bournemouth East Cemetery, Boscombe. F. 2. 124.

THE SINKING OF HMS *HAMPSHIRE* AND THE DEATH OF LORD KITCHENER (& NORMAN BARROW AND RALPH BUTLER)

HMS *Hampshire*, the armoured cruiser on which Norman Barrow was serving, fought in the battle of Jutland – a naval battle in which both the Germans and the British claimed victory. In fact, the death toll for the British was 6,907 men and for the Germans 2,545. Norman Barrow was lucky to escape – but fate was beckoning.

Immediately after the battle, HMS *Hampshire* was directed to carry Lord Kitchener from Scapa Flow on a diplomatic mission to Russia. Accordingly, the ship sailed for Archangel on 5 June 1916, carrying Field Marshal Lord Kitchener and all his staff.

Hampshire set off in a gale, and struck a mine shortly afterwards. It sank swiftly and of the 667 men on board only 12 survived. All the rest were drowned, including Lord Kitchener and Norman Barrow.

Today the wreck lies in 70 metres of water, upside down but largely intact, off the north-west coast of Orkney.

Bodies may well be found within it.

On attaining his 18th birthday, he joined the Army as a motor transport driver, but transferred to the Royal Naval Air Service as a cadet in January, 1918. In this capacity he developed great skill and ability, becoming a really brilliant airman, and gaining his commission as 2nd Lieutenant in the Royal Air Force. Two days before his death he had declined a post as Instructor, preferring active fighting work, and he was one of a selected few who were training for a new branch of aviation work. It was while engaged in this unfamiliar practice that he sustained the fall which proved fatal.

He was interred at Boscombe Cemetery on August 3rd, with full military honours, attended by a large concourse of his brother officers and other friends.

The school magazine, December 1918

Alfred William Bishop

Killed in action, 14 October 1918. Aged 20.
Rifleman, Rifle Brigade, attached 8th Battalion, City of London
Rifles.
Courrières Communal Cemetery, Pas de Calais, France.

He was... sent to France and was an active participator in that glorious
offensive which finally shattered Germany's hope of victory. In their
retreat, however, the enemy took a considerable toll of our men in the
advance guard, and amongst the number to fall was Bishop, killed by a
shell in the early morning of October 14th, near Courrières.

The school magazine, December 1918

Henry Richard Budden

Reported killed, 10 October 1915. Aged 20.
Lieutenant, 3rd Battalion. Dorset Regiment, attached to 2nd Lincolns.
White City Cemetery, Bois-Grenier, Nord, France. B. 14.

Soon after the outbreak of war he volunteered for service. On
November 1st, 1914, he obtained a commission in the 3rd Dorsets,
and left for France in March 1915, being attached to the 2nd Lincolns.
Not long afterwards he had a very narrow escape, a shrapnel shell
killed 14 men and wounding 7 others in a group of 25 men, amongst
whom Budden was standing.

On September 29th he was reported 'wounded, but remained at
duty.' This report seems to have been inaccurate, for on October
10th his guardian received a telegram from the War Office notifying
his death.

The school magazine, December 1915

Ronald Anderson Budden

Killed in action, 31 July 1917. Aged 19.
2nd Lieutenant, 1st Battalion, Worcestershire Regiment.
Ypres (Menin Gate) Memorial, Ypres, West-Vlaanderen, Belgium.
Panel 34.

Whilst undergoing the course of training at Sandhurst... in shooting he was extraordinarily efficient: in revolver practice he broke the College record and on the miniature range, with the rifle, he made a higher score than any other cadet.

The following description of the incident which terminated so fatally for poor Budden is extracted from a letter to his father written by Captain Urwick, of the Worcesters: –

'He was killed on the early morning of the 31st July, probably about 4 a.m. He was shot through the head by a German sniper and died instantly. He met his end in the most gallant fashion.

'The company of which his platoon formed part had already attacked and captured the front and second lines of the front trench system held by the enemy. While attacking the third line they were checked for a moment by machine-gun fire. Your son very promptly organised a small party from his platoon, and led them forward from shell-hole to shell-hole with a view to attacking and silencing the nearest of these machine-guns. While within point blank range of the gun he raised himself on the lip of the crater to throw a bomb, and was shot at that instant.

'The men with him immediately rushed the gun and bayoneted the crew, including the man who sniped your son. The gun was captured and the line went forward to its further objectives...'

The school magazine, December 1917

Armar Somerset Butler

Killed in action, October 1917. Aged 24.
Lieutenant, South Lancs Regiment, attached to RFC.
Sarigol Military Cemetery, Kriston, Greece. D. 584.

A.S. Butler and R.T. Butler, the sons of the Rev. Pierce Butler, of East
Stoke, Wareham, entered the school together, as boarders, in April,
1907.

Ralph, the younger brother, went down with HMS *Hampshire* in
June, 1916, and now his sorrowing parents have been called upon to
bear another loss, for they have received news that the elder brother,
Armar, was killed in the Balkans two months ago...

After eighteen months' service in the Balkans he was severely
wounded in the knee last Spring, and was for three months in hospital at Salonika. While there his Colonel wrote to him: 'I want you to
know how much the regiment and I think of your gallant leadership
and conduct.'

On his discharge he volunteered and was accepted for the RFC
[Royal Flying Corps]. Six weeks afterwards came the news that he had
been killed in action.

The school magazine, December 1917

Ralph Twisden Butler

Went down with HMS *Hampshire*, 5 June 1916. Aged 20.
Clerk, Royal Navy.
Lyness Royal Naval Cemetery, Orkney. F. 4.

Soon after leaving school he passed into the Navy as a Naval Clerk,
and he was an officer of HMS *Dublin* when the war broke out, being
given important work as officer in control of certain guns. He was with
that ship during the Dardanelles campaign.

Later on, having been transferred to HMS *Hampshire,* he came safely through the great naval battle off Jutland, when he was assistant observation officer in the foretop. Of this action he wrote: – 'I have been 70 hours in the foretop with only six hours' rest. It was a magnificent battle, and a privilege to have shared in it. I would not have missed it for worlds.'

The school magazine, July 1916

William Guy Fawcett Challis

Killed in action, 13 July 1916. Aged 24.
Lieutenant, 3rd Battalion, Hampshire Regiment.
Berks Cemetery Extension, Comines-Warneton, Hainaut, Belgium.
I.F. 19.

2nd Lieutenant H.M. Tollemache (another Old Boy of the same regiment) [who was later killed himself – see page 162] writes to Challis's sister: – 'You have heard of the death of your heroic brother. All the Regiment feel the deplorable loss. As we were at the Bournemouth School together I thought you would like an account of his brave deed prior to his death. He volunteered to go and fetch in the wounded in spite of heavy shell and machine gun fire. The other officer who accompanied him was killed. Challis managed to get back safely, only to be struck next day by a rifle grenade. He was killed instantly.'

The Chaplain says:– 'He lies buried in a soldiers' cemetery – the men made wreaths of flowers for his grave – all the officers of the Battalion available came to pay him their last respects.'

A few hours before his death Challis wrote home and described the bringing in of the wounded men from 'no man's land.' But – very characteristically – he omitted to state that it was he who brought them in.

The school magazine, July 1916

FIELD MARSHAL LORD KITCHENER (1850–1916)

Even today, the poster of the heavily-moustached officer pointing directly at us with the fierce message 'Your Country Needs You' is instantly memorable – having been reproduced and parodied countless times.

However, in the twenty-first century, the majority of us would probably find it hard to put a name to the officer depicted.

In fact, in 1914 it would have been recognised immediately as Lord Kitchener, Secretary of State for War, in charge of organising the large volunteer army that was necessary to fight Germany on the Western Front.

At the time of the outbreak of the First World War Kitchener was idolised. He had achieved fame for winning the Battle of Omdurman, 1898, thus securing control of the Sudan. This was the last battle at which the English Army made a cavalry charge, and Winston Churchill as a young subaltern took part in this, riding with the 21st Lancers.

Subsequently, Kitchener was made Lord Kitchener of Khartoum. His army career then took him to South Africa in the Boer War, Commander-in-Chief of the army in India, and Consul-General in Egypt. Honours were heaped on him: Knight of the Garter, Knight of St Patrick, Knight Grand Cross of the Order of the Bath, Order of Merit, Knight Grand Cross of the Order of the Star of India, Knight Grand Cross of the Order of St Michael and St George, and Knight Grand Cross of the Order of the Indian Empire.

Kitchener's loss at the sinking of HMS *Hampshire*, was seen as a tragedy of momentous importance. It has even been compared with the deaths of President J.F. Kennedy and Diana, Princess of Wales.

It has to said, however, that he was not popular with everyone, and Lloyd George acidly remarked, 'A good poster – but a poor general.'

Ralph William Cheshire

Died of wounds, 14 May 1918. Aged 19.
Private, Royal Berks Regiment.
Mont Huon Military Cemetery, Le Treport, Seine-Maritime, France.
VI. G. 3A.

Although engaged in numerous actions in the early spring [1918], he escaped unhurt until April 24th, when, in an attack on Kemmel Hill, he fell, wounded in many places. He was admitted to the 47th General Hospital at Le Treport and lingered there for three weeks. An operation was then performed, but without success, and he passed away on May 14th, 1918.

The school magazine, July 1918

Gordon Francis Collingwood

Killed in action, 28 March 1918. Aged 25.
Lieutenant, RGA.
Duisans British Cemetery, Etrun, Pas de Calais, France. V. F. 32.

In September, 1915, he obtained his commission as Lieutenant in the Army Service Corps, and, strangely enough, in that capacity he had to supply rations to the battery which his elder brother, Col. Collingwood, was commanding. Having applied for, and obtained, a transfer to the RGA., he was sent home for three months' training, and reached the French front again in May, 1917.

He served in Flanders through the battles of Messines and Ypres, and finally, on March 28, 1918, while serving his 6in. Howitzers, he fell, mortally wounded, in the defence of Arras. He is buried just outside that town

Gordon was the younger of two brothers educated here, sons of the late General Collingwood. The elder (Douglas) joined the Canadian Engineers; he attained the rank of major and won the Military Cross.

The school magazine, cutting from War Memorials of Bournemouth
School *(R. Coleman)*

Reginald Colborne

Believed killed in action, 30 October 1917. Aged 25.
Private, 29th London Regiment, Artists' Rifles OTC.
Poelcapelle British Cemetery, Langemark-Poelkapelle, West-Vlaanderen, Belgium. XVIII. A. 19.

... after an action at Passchendaele Ridge, he failed to answer to the roll. On that day it appears that he went 'over the top' with his platoon and was seen to be hit quite early in the action. The nature of the fighting precluded any attempt to give him help at the time, and it was hoped that he would find his way back to a dressing station. The hope proved false, and he was never again heard of. After a few weeks interval he was officially notified as 'missing' and now – a year later – as 'believed killed' on the day he disappeared.

The school magazine, December 1918

Cyril Henry Cooper

Killed in action, 6 April 1916. Aged 18.
2nd Lieutenant, Royal Garrison Artillery
Vlamertinghe Military Cemetery, Ypres, West-Vlaanderen, Belgium. III. B. 15.

He left for France on March 31st, joined his battery, 132nd Heavy Battery, Royal Garrison Artillery, on April 5th, and did his turn as orderly officer on his gun during the night. About 4 a.m. on the 6th the battery was heavily shelled by the Germans, and while Lieut. Cooper was in a shelter used as a battery commander's post working out a new range for his gun, the shelter received direct hits by several high explosive shells. He was killed instantaneously and buried in the debris. Several men of the BC staff were also buried but rescued alive. He was buried in the churchyard at Vlamertinghe the same day.

The school magazine, July 1916

Oliver Ipplefoot Cooper

Killed in action, 12 September 1918. Aged 20.
Private, Grenadier Guards.
Vaulx Hill Cemetery, Pas de Calais, France. II. G. 26.

On reaching military age Cooper joined the Grenadier Guards.

The sad news of his death in action was conveyed to Mrs Cooper by the Lieut. Colonel, who said: 'He died as he lived a true British soldier, who put his duty to his King and Country before any thought of his own personal safety.'

The school magazine, December 1918

Joseph Cornwell

Killed in action, 29 May 1916. Aged 24.
2nd Lieutenant, Royal Sussex Regiment.
Béthune Town Cemetery, Pas de Calais, France. III K. 18.

He had only eight days in the trenches and was looking forward to a rest when he was shot through the head by a sniper and died, without regaining consciousness. He was buried, next day, in the cemetery of Béthune.

The school magazine, December 1916

Horace Guy Croft

Killed in action, 8 August 1918. Aged 18.
Private, 7th Battalion, Royal Sussex Regiment.
Beacon Cemetery, Sailly-Laurette, Somme, France. V. C. 3.

On reaching military age his services were accepted by the Artists' Rifles OTC. He was enrolled in the 2nd Battalion on January 24th, 1918, and trained at Romford, Essex.

Having been transferred to the Sussex Regiment he was drafted to the Western Front in July. There, in his first engagement on August 8th, he fell, shot through the heart, death being instantaneous.

The school magazine, December 1918

Leonard Arthur Cuthbert MC

Killed in action, 20 December, 1919. Aged 21.
Captain, 2/19th Punjabis
Delhi Memorial, (India Gate), India. Face 2.

The recent fighting on the North-West Frontier of India has added one more to the long Roll of Honour of our Old Boys.

L.A. Cuthbert enlisted in the 2/7th Hants in September, 1914, at the early age of 16½ years, and proceeded with that regiment to India the following December. He was subsequently promoted to sergeant, and in May 1917, gazetted as a subaltern to the 2/19th Punjabis, with which regiment he saw active service in Palestine.

In a letter received from Major Sutherland of the 2/19th Punjabis, Mr and Mrs Cuthbert were informed that their son had been recommended for the MC for the gallantry during the fighting in which he fell. He was recommended for a MC for personal gallantry and leadership at Girvai, where he stopped a disorderly retirement by a dashing counter-attack, which proved such a sharp lesson to the enemy that his column retired unmolested.

His company formed the firing line of the attack that took, without a check, the hill at Mandanna Kach, on 20th December, which three regiments had failed to take the day before. He was sent with his company to occupy a piquet on the Mandanna Kach hill when the force retired. Shortly after the force retired, fire was opened on the piquet and a determined attack made on it by a strong force of Mahauds from all directions. Unfortunately, your gallant son was shot and killed early, and the piquet was rushed.

The school magazine, March 1920

J. M. Dawson

Accidentally killed, 7 September 1917. Aged 20.
Flight Officer, Royal Naval Air Service.
Coatham (Christ Church) Churchyard, Yorkshire. C. 13. 23.

... he joined the RNVR. Six months drill sufficed to qualify him as a fully-trained Able Seaman, whereupon he applied for a commission in the RNAS. He was gazetted in May, 1917, spent a month at the Crystal Palace undergoing instruction, and was then sent for further training to Redcar. There, when attempting his first solo flight, a fatal accident cut short his promising career.

He was buried with full naval honours, keenly regretted by all, officers and men alike...

The school magazine, December 1917

Harold Mackenzie Deans

Killed in action, 17 September 1918. Aged 24.
Captain, 7th/8th Battalion, King's Own Scottish Borderers.
Philosophe British Cemetery, Mazingarbe, Pas de Calais, France. III F. 24.

He was sent out to France in September, 1914, where he gained the Mons Star. He was badly wounded near La Bassée in November 1914, and was in hospital in Béthune when the Germans deliberately shelled it, killing many of the helpless inmates.

He went out again in March, 1915, and was with his regiment at the taking of Hill 60 on April 30th. In this engagement he was wounded for the second time, and badly 'gassed' also.

Less than two months afterwards we find him back once more, and throughout the winter of 1915–16 he was in the trenches in France and Belgium. It was during this trying season that he contracted the Trench Fever from which he never completely recovered. In spite of this he was in the trenches again through the year 1916 and into the following Spring, when he was invalided home. Whilst recuperating he took a 'gas course' in Scotland and passed so well that in the autumn of 1917 he was sent to America, with the British Mission, as Gas Instructor to the American Army. Having finished the course he returned to France last July, and was at once offered a renewal of his previous work for a period of six months. But by that time his health had so greatly improved, and he was feeling so much better, that he refused, saying 'it would not be playing the game to take on another "soft job" when fit men are wanted so badly at the Front'. So once more he went out, on August 24th.

On September 17th, Deans was in command of two Companies of the 7th and 8th KOSB detailed to make a raid on the enemy trenches. He had reached the German support line, where he was to establish his Headquarters, but seeing his men on the right flank to be held up by heavy machine-gun fire, he ran forward, rallied the men, and himself led them in a charge towards the next trench. Near this he fell, shot by a bullet from a machine-gun.

The school magazine, December 1918

Herbert Leslie Durham

Killed in action at the Dardanelles, 6 September 1915. Aged 21.
Lance Corporal, 1st Battalion, Lancashire Fusiliers.
Azmak Cemetery Suvla Turkey. I B. 16.

He joined the 3rd Sherwood Foresters and Derby Regiment in November, 1914, and, after being transferred to the Lancashire Fusiliers, he was sent out to the Dardanelles last August. He fell on September 6th – killed in action.

The school magazine, December 1915

Reverdy Cecil Dyason

Died from gas-shell poisoning, 19 September 1918. Aged 20.
Lance Bombadier, 116th Battery, RFA.
Terlincthun British Cemetery Wimille, Pas de Calais, France. III.F.38.

In October, 1917, he crossed to France with his Battery, which formed part of a Brigade of RFA moving to different parts of the Western Front, as circumstances required. About the middle of September 1918, he was acting as Brigade Orderly for his Battery at his Brigade Headquarters when the Germans got a direct hit on it with gas shell. In consequence of this, the Colonel, Adjutant, and all the rest of the staff (including Dyason) were badly 'gassed'. Dyason was taken to the General Hospital at Boulogne on September 16th and died there three days afterwards. He was buried, with full military honours, on the 20th.

The school magazine, December 1918

Howard George Henry Farwell

Killed in action, 9 August 1916. Aged 27.
Lance Corporal, 2nd Battalion, Hampshire Regiment.
Potijze Burial Ground Cemetery, Ypres, West-Vlaanderen, Belgium. T. 1.

He enlisted in the Hants Regiment and started with them for India, but falling sick he was left in hospital at Alexandria. When sent home later on he was transferred to another battalion of the Hants Regiment. With them he went to Egypt, and after service in the Dardanelles and Salonika, he was sent to France, where he was killed on August 9th.

The school magazine, December 1916

Harold Walter Finch

Died of wounds, 26 November 1916. Aged 21.
Sergeant, 2nd Battalion, Hampshire Regiment.
Grove Town Cemetery, Meaulte, Somme, France. II.K.12.

In one of the numerous battles which took place near the banks of the Somme in November it appears he was dangerously wounded in the legs and the body. As soon as possible he was removed to the London Casualty Clearing Station, where everything possible was done for him, but he passed away – quietly and without apparent pain – early on Sunday morning, November 26th.

The school magazine, December 1916

Howard Grimley Floyd

Killed in action, 9 April 1918. Aged 20.
2nd Lieutenant, 1st/5th Battalion, Devonshire Regiment.
Ramleh War Cemetery, Israel. T. 13.

He sailed for Egypt in January, 1918, and was killed in action, in Palestine, about ten weeks after leaving England.

In sending the sad details to his mother, Lieut. Colonel H.V. Bastow, who was in command, says: –

'I am deeply grieved to have to let you know your son was killed in action on the night of April 9th. Poor boy! It was very sad that one so young should be cut off so early, and he was such a very promising young officer – very popular with his brother officers and his Company. It may be some relief to you to know I was with him when he died and he cannot have suffered any pain as death was practically instantaneous. He was hit by a machine gun bullet behind the ear and through the neck.

I had sent 3 Companies at about 2 p.m. to take a village situated on a high hill. This was accomplished by a magnificent bayonet charge at 4 o'clock. Then at dusk we had to consolidate the position, which was commanded and enfiladed on all sides by machine guns posted on the surrounding hills. Your poor boy was posting his outposts at 7 p.m., when he came under severe machine gun fire and dropped practically at once. We carried him in and gave him brandy, but life had already expired.

The school magazine, July 1918

Harold William Froud

Died of wounds, 27 July 1917. Aged 28.
2nd Lieutenant, 5th Battalion, Durham Light Infantry.
Achiet-le-Grand Communal Cemetery Extension, Pas de Calais, France. I. K. 10.

He gave up his work to enlist in the Artists' Rifles OTC and was in due course 'gazetted'. Ordered to the Western Front in July, 1916, he was wounded the following September, but rejoined his unit less than two months afterwards. An attack of trench fever put him again on the sick list and necessitated his spending some time in the South of France, recuperating. Once more he went up to the line, but it was not long before he received his call. He fell, mortally wounded, whilst making a raid on a German trench.

The school magazine, December 1917

Frank Ernest Game

Died from shell-gas poisoning, 7 June 1918. Aged 21.
Private, S. Staffordshire Infantry.
Pernes British Cemetery, Pas de Calais, France. II. F. 35.

... he was included in a large draft transferred to the Tank Corps, but the bulk of the men proving 'wash-outs' so far as the Tanks particular requirements were concerned, he shared in the general fate of being transferred to the South Staffordshire Infantry, and although on the discovery of his ability the Tank Corps made strenuous endeavour to get him returned, the effort was fruitless.

The Unit to which he was posted, being a Training Battalion, afforded no possibility of promotion, and his Colonel, who desired to recommend him for a Commission, was precluded from so doing by a War Office order limiting such recommendations to men with overseas experience. Game, however, as cheerful and willing in the lowest position as in the highest, and on completion of his training he left for France on April 3rd, receiving the poisonous gas which caused his death in the night of May 21/22, after only seven weeks at the front.

Removed to a Casualty Station, he never recovered sufficiently to be taken further, though, after being totally blind for four days, he regained his sight and was able to write home a little note. There seemed then some hope of his recovery, but the improvement was not maintained, and after 17 days' suffering he passed away.

The school magazine, July 1918

Oliver Goldsmith

Died at Tidworth, 5 January 1916. Aged 17.
Trooper, Hants Yeomanry.
Bournemouth (Wimborne Road) Cemetery, Dorset. 1. 3. 18 N.

The cause of death was septic poisoning, following an accidental wound to the hand. He was in hospital only three days, but in spite of every care he succumbed at the end of that time, the poison having attacked the tissues of the throat and tonsils.

The school magazine, March 1916

Clarence Cecil Goodall

Killed in action, 7 July 1916. Aged 25.
2nd Lieutenant, 3rd Battalion, Dorset Regiment.
Serre Road Cemetery No. 2, Somme, France. XVII. F. 6.

In July, 1915, he was appointed to a commission in the 3rd Dorsets, where he did valuable work as a musketry instructor. He was married on December 1st, 1915, and went to the front [France] on March 17th, 1916.

His officer commanding his regiment writes that he 'was killed in action on July 7th whilst gallantly leading his platoon in an attack. He was hit in the neck and killed instantly, so did not suffer in any way.

The school magazine, July 1916

Claude Graham

Died, 13 November 1916. Aged 23.
Private, Hampshire Regiment.
Alexandria (Hadra) War Memorial Cemetery, Egypt. D. 69.

He joined the Army nearly two years ago and went with the Hampshire Regiment to India. In the Autumn of 1915 he volunteered, and was accepted, for service in Mesopotamia, and from December 2nd until the capitulation he was one of the defending force at Kut, when he became a prisoner of war. After spending four months in hospital at Baghdad he was exchanged and sent to hospital at Bombay. On October 26th he left Bombay for Alexandria, where he arrived on November 8th. He wrote quite cheerfully the next day and appeared to be making good progress, but two days later he had an attack of malaria, which proved fatal on November 13th.

The school magazine, December 1916

William Herbert Gunning

Died of wounds, 31 October 1916. Aged 23.
2nd Lieutenant, Hampshire Regiment.
Pieta Military Cemetery, Malta. D. XV. 2.

When war broke out he took a commission in the Hampshire Regiment, and, having been ordered to the Near East about a year ago, he came in for some heavy fighting in the Balkan Peninsula.

A report from Alexandria stated that he had been wounded on October 1st, and a letter was received from him stating that he was going on very well and that his friends were not to worry. 'It was exactly a week ago that I was hit,' he wrote. 'Last Sunday at 2.30 a.m. I got one in the side of the head, but fortunately I was wearing a shrapnel helmet and the bullet did not touch my skull. I shall try and send the helmet home; it will be worth keeping, for it saved my life. I was operated on Tuesday as the wound wasn't too clean. There were two holes on the right side of my head where the bullet passed through, but they have cut them into one.' He added that he was feeling 'like a two-year old.' On October 28th he sailed for Malta. Five days later news was received that he was 'dangerously wounded with gun-shot wound in the head,' and his death was announced the next day.

The school magazine, December 1916

Arthur William Hame

Killed in action, 21 May 1918. Aged 26.
Captain, RFA.
Soissons Memorial, Aisne, France.

(Details of Hame's death are unknown. He was killed in action in France, after 3½ years. His name is recorded on the British Memorial at Soissons, listed among nearly 4,000 British soldiers who have no known graves.)

Leslie Hickman Hands

Died of wounds, 4 March 1917. Aged 21.
Royal Fusiliers.
St Sever Cemetery Extension, Rouen, Seine-Maritime, France.
O. VII. E. 1.

... in January 1916, he joined the Bankers' Battalion of the Royal Fusiliers. After periods of training at Loughton (Essex) and Portobello (Edinburgh) he was detailed for service on the Western Front last July. There, after going through several engagements in the Battles of the Somme, he was severely wounded in action on February 17th. The wound unfortunately proved to be fatal, and he died in a French hospital on March 4th.

The school magazine, April 1917

Cecil Ernest Harbord

Killed in action, 26 September 1916. Aged 20.
Hants Cyclists (Transferred to the Dorset Regiment).
Thiépval Memorial, Somme, France. Pier and Face 7 B

Harbord was reported 'missing' on 26 September, 1916. It now, unfortunately, appears to be clear, from a letter written to Mr and Mrs Harbord by the OC their son's Company, that he was killed in action on that day.

The school magazine, April 1917

Sadly, Cecil Harbord is one of the thousands of combatants whose bodies were never found or identified. His name is among the 72,090 names carved on the impressive Thiépval Memorial, listing those who have no known grave.

Douglas George Hazard

Killed in action, 25 May 1915. Aged 21.
Lieutenant, 2nd Battalion, Shropshire Light Infantry.
Sanctuary Wood Cemetery, Ypres, West-Vlaanderen, Belgium.
V. U. 13.

Describing the action which appears to have cost poor Hazard his life, Major R.T. Toke, 1st Welsh Regiment, writes: 'On the 25th May we made a night attack about three miles east of Ypres. We attacked through a small wood and up a hill. I led my men amid a murderous fire and charged the trench at the top and took it. The Germans retired to a trench about 15 yards further back and fired very heavily on us. While lying here a Company of the Shropshires, who were supporting us, came charging through the wood led by an officer (probably Lieutenant Hazard). He was at the head of the Company shouting to them to 'Charge.' I got up and shouted to my own men to 'Charge.' I then saw the Shropshire officer fall, but it was too dark to see whether he was killed or wounded, and the fire was so heavy that I could not get near him. We hung on until dawn, until I had only about 30 men left. We then retired under a most murderous fire.

THE THIÉPVAL MEMORIAL TO THE MISSING OF THE SOMME

The appalling carnage of the Battle of the Somme is commemorated by a huge memorial, designed by Sir Edwin Lutyens, near the village of Thiépval, about thirteen miles (21km) north-east of Amiens.

The memorial is in the form of a gigantic arch, 150 feet (46m) high, with sixteen piers of red brick faced with Portland stone engraved with the names of the 72,090 men whose bodies were completely lost in the Somme battles between July 1916 and March 1918. Most of these unlucky men died in the first Battle of the Somme, between 1 July and 4 November 1916.

No one can fail to be deeply moved by the thought of so many lives so needlessly lost. At the end of the first day of the Battle of the Somme – 1 July 1916 – the British Army had suffered 60,000 casualties, one for every 18 inches of the front.

Carved on the Thiépval Memorial are the words:

> Here are recorded named of officers and men of the
> British Armies who fell on the Somme battlefields
> July 1915 February 1918 but to whom the fortune of
> war denied the known and honoured burial given to
> their comrades in death

'Your son fell within 15 yards of the German trenches. We tried to get back through the wood after dark to bring in the wounded, but could only get half-way up, as the Germans were again in position.'

The school magazine, March 1916

Walter Reginald Hazel

Died of malaria, 18 October 1918. Aged 21.
Lance Corporal, Royal Wiltshire Yeomanry.
Damascus Commonwealth War Cemetery, Syria. A. 48.

After training in Sussex he went to France with the British Expeditionary Force, and had two years' fighting, finishing with the Battle of the Somme. In this action he was severely wounded, and it took him three months at Netley Hospital to recuperate. His next move was to Aldershot, where he won his crossed swords and guns.

Proceeding later on to Egypt with the EEF (in which he was attached to the Sherwood Rangers Yeomanry), he was there only a few weeks before he succumbed to an attack of malaria on October 18th, 1918.

The school magazine, December 1918

Charles Alfred Heather

Killed in action, 5 July 1915. Aged 20.
Private, 8th Battalion, Australian Infantry, AIF.
Shrapnel Valley Cemetery, Turkey. II. C. 28.

Some time after leaving School, Heather's family emigrated to Australia, and we lost touch with him until we heard that on the outbreak of the war he had at once given up his career to join the First Australian Expeditionary Force. He left Melbourne for Egypt on October 20th last year. On July 5th it appears that he was in a dug-out when a shell burst some yards away. A fragment hit Heather in the neck, killing him instantly.

The school magazine, December 1915

Edward Robert Eyre Hickling

Died of wounds, *c.* 2 November 1914. Aged 19.
1st Lieutenant, 3rd Battalion, Gloucestershire Regiment.
Poperinge Communal Cemetery, Poperinge, West-Vlaanderen,
Belgium. I. B. 8.

We give below as extract from a letter written by an officer in his
company, which shows the kind of enemy our men have to deal with: –

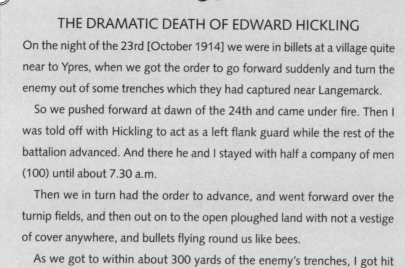

THE DRAMATIC DEATH OF EDWARD HICKLING

On the night of the 23rd [October 1914] we were in billets at a village quite near to Ypres, when we got the order to go forward suddenly and turn the enemy out of some trenches which they had captured near Langemarck.

So we pushed forward at dawn of the 24th and came under fire. Then I was told off with Hickling to act as a left flank guard while the rest of the battalion advanced. And there he and I stayed with half a company of men (100) until about 7.30 a.m.

Then we in turn had the order to advance, and went forward over the turnip fields, and then out on to the open ploughed land with not a vestige of cover anywhere, and bullets flying round us like bees.

As we got to within about 300 yards of the enemy's trenches, I got hit just above the knee and was of course to all intents and purposes 'down and out.' But I yelled to Hickling to take the men on – whether he heard me or not I cannot say – but I saw him afterwards running forwards with his men, and I was told later that he got through all right.

Then I lay there for about seven or eight hours, unable to move, until some ambulance people came along about 4 p.m. and took me back on a stretcher. When I got back I heard that Hickling had been badly shot in the hip, and though the details are not nice perhaps you would rather know them.

It appears that we captured a lot of German prisoners and he was detailed to bring a party of them back.

He had guard on them, with fixed bayonets, and of course all the Germans were disarmed, but it appears that the German officer who was with them had a revolver which had not been taken from him, and while poor young Hickling took his eyes off him for a moment, this swine turned round and deliberately shot him.

In the space of two or three seconds that German officer had been simply hacked to ribbons by our men's bayonets, but alas that didn't save poor Hickling. It was altogether a most tragic affair.

Poor Hickling lingered on in hospital for a few days, but passed away about November 2nd at Boulogne.

Edwin Arundel Hill MC

Died of wounds, 26 October 1918. Aged 23.
Major, 8th Battalion, Royal Sussex Regiment.
Villers-Bretonneux Military Cemetery, Somme, France. XVIA. B. 20.

Hill was only 19 years old when the war broke out, but, horrified by the atrocities perpetrated by the German troops who invaded Belgium, he enlisted, without delay, in the Royal Sussex Regiment... very soon after reaching the age of 23 he was gazetted Major. In England's darkest hour, when, in the spring of this year, our forces were beaten back by sheer weight of numbers, Hill was in the thick of the fighting. On at least one occasion his regiment was nearly surrounded, and it was only after a desperate struggle that the enemy were driven off. In October last it fell to his lot to command the Battalion, his superior officer having contracted influenza, and it was while returning by motor-car from an inspection of the front line that he received the wounds from which he died.

It appears that a shell burst immediately underneath the car, blowing it to pieces and gravely injuring the inmates. Hill was taken to the base for treatment, an operation was successfully performed and he seemed likely to recover, when 'gas gangrene' set in, and, with fatal rapidity, carried off the patient. Mention should be made of the heroism of Pte. James Smith who volunteered himself for the operation of transfusion of blood, which was attempted, though without success.

He was mentioned in dispatches by Sir Douglas Haig, and was recommended for the Military Cross, a decoration which (alas!) he did not live to receive.

The school magazine, December 1918

Fred Oswald Hodges

Killed in the First Battle of Gaza, 26 March 1917. Aged 31.
Sergeant, 1st/4th Battalion, Cheshire Regiment
Gaza War Cemetery, Israel. XXVIII. D. 14.

F.O. Hodges was one of those who entered [Bournemouth School] on the opening day.

He joined the Cheshire Regiment in April 1915, was sent in due course to the Dardanelles, and took part in the landing at Suvla Bay.

Early in 1916 he was invalided to Egypt, and – on his recovery – he rejoined his unit then on the way to Palestine. In the spring of 1917 they came into contact with the Turks, and Hodges fell during the first attack on Gaza.

The Captain of his Company in a letter to Mr Hodges said: 'It is with deep regret that I have to write and tell you about your son's death. He was in the first line of my Company on March 26 when we attacked the Turks at Gaza. Sergeant Hodges led his men in a most gallant way, being hit in the mouth, when only about 200 yards from the position, and killed instantly.

The school magazine, March 1920

Horace Lloyd Holland

Drowned at sea, 21 February 1920. Aged 21.
Flying Officer, RAF
Hollybrook Memorial, Southampton.

Greatly interested in aeronautics, he took a course of instruction in flying (soon after leaving school) at the Bournemouth Aerodrome, and – in his early efforts – he had at least one very narrow escape from premature death.

... in due course was gazetted to a commission in the Royal Air Force.

He was engaged on night-patrol in the defence of London, and took part in repelling the last air raid on the night of Whit-Sunday, 1918.

The school magazine, March 1920

It will be noted that Holland in fact did not die during the war. He survived, serving in the RAF, but was drowned in the Irish Sea when his aircraft inexplicably fell from the sky. Writing his obituary, Dr Fenwick wrote, 'Holland died in the performance of his duty, and we sadly give him that place on our Roll of Honour which is so justly his due.'

Henry Joseph Hollies

Killed in action, France, 16 September 1916. Aged 26.
Corporal, County of London Regiment.
London Cemetery and Extension, Longueval, Somme, France. 1A. B. 30.

... went to France with his battalion in the Spring of 1915. Later in the year he was wounded and sent home, but he returned to the front early in 1916. He had leave again in April, and visited Bournemouth, being then in splendid health, but not many months after rejoining he fell as noted above.

The school magazine, December 1916

Cyril James Horsey

Died of wounds received in action, 22 November 1916. Aged 25.
2nd Lieutenant, 7th Battalion South Lancs Regiment.
St Sever Cemetery, Rouen, Seine-Maritime, France. B. 2. 4.

In August, 1916, he went to France, attached, as Bombing Officer, to the 7th Battalion, South Lancashire Regiment. Three months later, during an action in which he took part on November 18th, he was wounded by gunfire in the leg, but owing to heavy shelling several hours elapsed before he received any attention. Eventually, he was brought in and taken to No. 2 Red Cross Hospital, Rouen, where he arrived in a state of exhaustion. From this condition he never really rallied, and he died of his wound (and the subsequent exposure) on November 22nd.

Besides his mother and sister, he leaves a widow and a little daughter (born some months after his death) to mourn his loss.

The school magazine, December 1917

George Ede Hunt

Accidentally killed, 21 July 1918. Aged 20.
2nd Lieutenant, RAF
Coatham (Christ Church) Churchyard, Yorkshire. C. 9. 11.

On leaving school he was appointed to an Officer Cadet Battalion, was gazetted in due course to the KOYLI, and sent to the Western Front. There he had two wonderful escapes, being twice buried by shells bursting so close as to kill most of the men at his vicinity, but on returning to England as a 'casualty' he made a very good recovery. When convalescent he obtained a transfer to the Royal Air Force, visited the school before proceeding to his new quarters and again (on July 17th) during a 'leave'. Five days later we got the tragic news that he had been accidentally killed while flying at Stonehenge.

The school magazine, December 1918

John Dorrington Ingram

Died at Armentières, 16 January, 1915. Aged 24.
Queen's Own Westminsters.
Cité Bonjean Military Cemetery, Armentières, Nord, France. IX. A. 81.

... he joined the Queen's Westminster Rifles. After being in London for a week or two, they were sent into camp at Hemel Hempstead, where they remained until they were quite suddenly ordered to the front. They appear to have gone to the front very shortly after arriving in France, and had a very arduous time in the trenches, which, from his letters, were, particularly at that time, a veritable quagmire. However, like the men they were, they made the best of it. On the fatal day he was in a spot where the enemy were particularly active in sniping. The General and the Brigade-Major came along the trench to visit it, and as they were passing Ingram a shot wounded him very severely in the head, and only just missed the General. He lived for four days, but never regained consciousness, and was buried on January 17th in the Military Cemetery at Armentières.

The school magazine, March 1915

Frank Sparshatt Jefferis

Died, 14 November 1918. Aged 18.
Cadet, 'D' Coy, 3rd Battalion, Hampshire Regiment.
Bournemouth (Wimborne Road) Cemetery, Dorset. B. 7. 13. N.

THE BIRTH OF THE ROYAL AIR FORCE

George Hunt, whose accidental death is noted on pages 141–142, must have been one of the first 2,073 recruits of the newly-formed Royal Air Force. In fact, the RAF was only four months old when he crashed his aircraft near Stonehenge.

In August 1917, the South African statesman General Jan Smuts had presented a report to the War Council on the future of air power. He noted the huge potential in air warfare, and recommended that a new air service should be formed, on a level with the army and the Royal Navy.

Accordingly, on 1 April 1918, the Royal Flying Corps and the Royal Naval Air Service were amalgamated to form a completely new branch of the armed forces – to be called 'The Royal Air Force'.

It is interesting to see that George Ede Hunt is listed as being '2nd Lieutenant' – a rank which would soon be changed to 'Flight Lieutenant'.

At the time of George Hunt's death, the RAF did not possess or use parachutes – so it must have taken great courage to fly those early aeroplanes.

The death of F.S. Jefferis touches us more closely than that of any other Old Boy whom the exigencies of the war have taken from us. Six weeks before he died he was still in our midst, a Prefect and an honoured member of the school...

Having been appointed to an Officer Cadet Battalion (Royal Engineers) he at once proceeded to Newark to join his unit. Whilst there he was attacked by influenza, followed by septic pneumonia, and, although he made a brave fight, seeming indeed at one time quite likely to recover, an intervening relapse found him in such an enfeebled state that nothing could save him, and he passed away, unconscious, on Thursday November 14th.

The school magazine, December 1918

Percy James Johnson

Drowned at sea, 4 October 1918. Aged 27.
Civilian

[Percy was employed by the Royal Siamese Education Department and had returned to England on leave. He was returning to Bangkok when his ship, the Japanese liner *Hirano Maru*, was torpedoed.]

The ship was torpedoed by an enemy submarine at 6 o'clock in the morning of October 4th, about 60 miles off the South Coast of Ireland, and sank in seven minutes, only eleven passengers being saved.

Johnson's elder (and only) brother was killed in Egypt in 1915.

The school magazine, December 1918

Unfortunately, the death of Johnson's brother does not appear in the school magazine – nor on the school's War Memorial.

Aaron Norton Clulee Jones

Died of pneumonia, 8 October 1918. Aged 18.
Cadet, RAF
King's Norton (St Nicholas) Churchyard, Warwickshire.
West Extension, 2481.

He entered [the Royal Air Force] on September 10th, 1918, having passed the qualifying examination.

After a few days' training at Hastings, he was sent to West Sandling Camp, Folkestone. During the removal the weather was very bad, Spanish Influenza broke out and wrought havoc with the cadets. Jones unfortunately contracted the epidemic. It was followed in his case by Pneumonia, and he died – on October 8th – the day following his 18th birthday.

The school magazine, December 1918

Francis William Kelly

Killed in action, 12 January 1917. Aged 23.
Wiltshire Regiment.
Amara War Cemetery, Iraq. XVIII. C. 12.

... he enlisted in the Hants, being afterwards transferred to the Wiltshire Regiment. With them he went out to the Persian Gulf, where he was killed in action on January 12th, 1917.

The school magazine, April 1917

Frank Eric Kent

Killed in action, 11 September 1917. Aged 19.
Gunner, RFA, 200th Brigade, B Battery.
Duhallow A.D.S. Cemetery, Ypres, West-Vlaanderen, Belgium. I. C. 23.

After a period of training at Cosham he went on draft to France in February, 1917, and was put into a 'Flying' column. The work here was very strenuous. Heavy guns had to be continually moved, generally at very short notice, and often in the middle of the night, to support infantry advances at various parts of the line...

On September 11th the enemy began to fire gas shells into his Battery, and the very first fell into the gun pit where Kent was. The men had no time to put on their gas masks and Kent was himself so badly 'gassed' that he died in the ambulance without regaining consciousness.

The school magazine, December 1917

Lewis John Kent (formerly Goss-Chalk)

Killed in action, 13 July 1916. Aged 19.
Private, 14th Battalion, London Scottish Regiment.
Maroeuil British Cemetery, Pas de Calais, France. III. A. 14.

On the action which cost him his life a Press correspondent wrote: –
'On the right the London Scottish were holding on to their redoubt,
building barricades, and beating off the German bombers. But as the
hours passed ammunition became scarce. The supplies of bombs here
and there were almost exhausted. The London men went about collecting German bombs, and for some time these served, but not enough
could be found to maintain effective fire. The position became more
ugly. But the men did not lose heart. In those bad hours there were
many men who showed great qualities of courage, and were great cap-
tains whatever their rank.'

His friend, who was with him at the last states that they were in the
front trenches, on guard, and that when Jack's turn came to watch he
said, 'Keep down, you fellows; there is no need for more than one of
us to go under.' They were being heavily bombarded when an aerial
torpedo burst over him. He was not actually hit, but killed instantaneously by the shock.

The school magazine, April 1917

Thomas Wilkes Lonsdale, MC

Killed in action, 5 June 1916. Aged 22.
Captain, 7th Battalion, Duke of Cornwall's Light Infantry.
Longuenesse (St Omer) Souvenir Cemetery, Pas de Calais, France. II. C. 2.

When war broke out he obtained a commission in the 7th Battn.
DCLI. He was sent to France a year ago, was soon afterwards given his
'second star,' and promoted to be captain last spring.

He has been mentioned in dispatches and verbally complimented, with his company, by the Officer Commanding his Division.

On May 24th, in circumstances not yet published, he was shot in the abdomen and died from his wound on June 5th.

The school magazine, July 1916

Ernest Gerald Marshall

Killed in action, 24 September 1918. Aged 25.
Sergeant, Hants RGA.
Hermies Hill British Cemetery, Pas de Calais, France. I. H. 20.

When the war broke out he at once determined to abandon his civil occupation and join the Army. This he did in October, 1914, enlisting in the Hants RGA. Promotion came to him in due course, in recognition of his merit, and he had attanted to the highest grade of non-commissioned rank when, on September 24th [1918] he was killed in action two days after his return to France at the expiry of a short 'leave'.

Marshall fought in the Palestine campaign as well as on the Western theatre of war.

The school magazine, December 1918

Charles Stanley Martin

Killed in action, 4 October 1917. Aged 26.
2nd Lieutenant, 6th Battalion, Leicester Regiment.
Bedford House Cemetery, Ypres, West-Vlaanderen, Belgium.
Enclosure No. 2. I. E. 36.

On October 4th, when on the way to join in the Ypres battle, a long range enemy shell landed at the head of his company. Martin's platoon was leading, and he was walking with the Company Commander. Both were instantaneously killed with 6 other men and 5 were wounded.

The school magazine, December 1917

Harold Henry Martyn

Killed in action, 21 March 1918. Aged 20.
Captain, 2nd Wiltshires.
Pozières Memorial, Somme, France. Panel 64.

He was trained at Sandhurst, attached to the 2nd Wilts Regiment, and went to France in May, 1916, at the age of 18. He was immediately engaged in some very severe fighting, taking part in the battle of Loos, and of Trones Wood in July 1916. His regiment was afterwards congratulated by Sir Douglas Haig on the magnificent work they had done.

Later on he was appointed Instructor in a Lewis Machine Gun School in France, and continued in that capacity until November, 1917, when re-joined this regiment with promotion to Captain's rank.

The following spring saw the beginning of the last great German offensive, when, in trying to stem the adverse tide, so many of our gallant men deliberately chose to die rather than surrender. On that day, March 21st, he was with his regiment holding the front line near St Quentin when the enemy attacked in great force. His unit was isolated and became surrounded by the hostile horde, but kept on fighting to the last, when Martyn was seen to fall, shot in the head by a machine gun bullet.

The school magazine, December 1918

WRITING TO CONSOLE GRIEVING PARENTS

Commanding Officers had an emotionally demanding task, as they wrote back to the grieving parents of young men who had been killed. In view of the enormous number of casualties, this letter-writing must have taken a great deal of time. Here is part of a letter to the parents of Charles Stanley Martin *(see pages 147–148)* written by the Lieutenant Colonel of his Battalion:

On October 1st he had been with the Company when ordered to reinforce the line. The Company went forward through very heavy shell fire and he acted splendidly, and came out through it again fit and well. In July, when raiders were called for from the Battalion to raid the German trenches, he was one of the officers who volunteered. He worked very hard and patrolled many nights, and, if the raid had come off, he would have won an honour.

So it was, he got the Major General's honour card, which I hope you saw when he was on leave last. The whole Battalion mourns his loss.

John Hayes May

Killed in action, 20 November 1917. Aged 21.
2nd Lieutenant, Queen Victoria Rifles.
Hermies Hill British Cemetery, Pas de Calais, France. I. H. 27.

In May, 1916, he went with his unit to France and took part in the great 'push' which came two months later [the Battle of the Somme]. Suffering from trench fever in the autumn, he was invalided home and remained for a considerable time in this country, receiving his commission in July 1917. Six week later, on the Cambrai front, he was killed instantaneously by the explosion of a shell.

The school magazine, March 1918

Hermann Watling Meyer

Went down with HMS *Queen Mary*, 31 May 1916. Aged 20.
Engine Room Artificer, RN.
Portsmouth Naval Memorial. 15

In the early stage of the war he was on HMS *Queen Mary* before the
great Naval Battle off Jutland, when his ship was hit and sank in so
short a time that practically none of the crew were rescued.

Alfred George Mills

Died, 10 August 1915. Aged 17.
Private, 10th Battalion, Hampshire Regiment.
Helles Memorial, Turkey. Panel 125–134, or 223–226, 228–229 & 328

It was announced more than a year ago that he was missing on 10th
August 1915, and, no news having been received of him since then, it
is presumed that he was killed.

The school magazine, December 1916

The Helles Memorial, in Turkey, commemorates the whole of the
Gallipoli campaign, so far as the forces of the Commonwealth were concerned in it, and in particular it displays the names of over 20,000 of
those with no known grave.

Frank Leslie Moorey

Died of wounds, 19 February 1915. Aged 20.
Private, 13th Kensington Battalion, County of London Regiment.
Kensington (Hanwell) Cemetery, Middlesex. 170. 5.

THE NAVAL BATTLE OF JUTLAND, 1916

The Battle of Jutland, fought off the Jutland Peninsula on 31st May 1916, was the largest naval engagement of the First World War. It was inconclusive – but naturally both sides claimed victory.

In fact, the British lost fourteen ships – three battle cruisers (including HMS *Queen Mary*, with Hermann Meyer on board), three armoured cruisers, and eight destroyers – whereas the Germans lost only ten ships – one battle cruiser, four light cruisers, and five torpedo-boats. In terms of manpower, the British suffered 6,094 men killed, 510 wounded, and 177 captured; the German losses totalled 2,551 men killed and 507 wounded.

Nevertheless, the result of the Battle of Jutland was that the British retained control of the North Sea, while the German surface fleet remained in their home ports for the rest of the war, only making use of their U-boats to threaten British shipping.

It is worth noting that the 21-year-old Duke of York, the future King George VI, also took part in this battle, serving on board HMS *Collingwood*. He wrote home: 'It was certainly a great experience to have been through and it shows that we are at war and that the Germans can fight if they like.'

... after about three months' training his regiment was sent out to the front and into the trenches at La Bassée. Moorey was wounded on November 18th, but soon recovered and went back to the trenches. Whilst in a 'dug-out' there, a German shell exploded near him, filling his mouth and nose with clay. A germ in this clay set up an abscess in the throat, leading to septic pneumonia, from which he died on February 19th.

The school magazine, March 1915

William Edward Moorey

Killed in action, 26 October 1917. Aged 26.
2nd Lieutenant, 3rd Battalion, London Regiment.
Tyne Cot Memorial, Zonnebeke, West-Vlaanderen, Belgium. Panel 148.

... he enlisted in the Royal Fusiliers and in due course he went to France on active service with his Battalion, from June, 1915, to July, 1916, being wounded at Contalmaison.

He was promoted to a commission last May and joined his unit at the front in June.

... his brother Leslie, another Old Boy, died of wounds in February, 1915.

The school magazine, December 1917.

Arthur Roy Mosley

Died of wounds, 23 November 1917. Aged 22.
Lieutenant, King's Own Yorkshire Light Infantry.
Rocquigny-Equancourt Road British Cemetery, Manancourt, Somme, France. III. B. 15.

In January, 1917, he went out to France with his battalion. He first went into action in February at Beaumont Hamel, and afterwards took part in the big 'push' of last May. Shell shock and a slight wound (the result of that engagement) necessitated his removal to hospital and rest camp for a period of six weeks. In the autumn, after a short 'leave' he again went into the trenches, and on November 20th, his Captain having been fatally wounded, Mosley was instructed to lead his company in a very important attack. It was whilst engaged in carrying out this order that he received the wound which proved fatal.

The school magazine, March 1918

Brian Brooke New

Killed in action, 16 August 1917. Aged 26.
2nd Lieutenant, Duke of Cornwall's Light Infantry (Special Reserve).
Tyne Cot Memorial, Zonnebeke, West-Vlaanderen, Belgium. Panel 80 to 82 and 163A.

On the outbreak of war he joined the 7th Hants Territorials and went with them to India, where he was promoted to the rank of Corporal. Rather more than a year ago he returned to join an Officer Cadet Battalion in England, being gazetted soon afterwards to the DCLI. In March, 1917, he went to France as signal officer to his Company.

In the action which cost him his life there was a successful advance, and it became necessary to move the signalling station forward. Whilst carrying out this movement, 'Barry' and a private who was with him, were instantaneously killed by the bursting of a shell.

The school magazine, December 1917

John Douglas Nutman

Killed in action, 31 August 1918. Aged 19.
Private, 2nd/4th Battalion, Oxford and Bucks Light Infantry.
Aval Wood Military Cemetery, Vieux-Berquin, Nord, France. III. A. 3.

Originally in the Dorset Regiment, he was transferred to the Devons, and, on proceeding to France last March, he was drafted into the Oxford and Bucks. He was reported 'Killed in action' on 31st August 1918, but no details have come to hand.

The school magazine, December 1918

Leslie Alfred Okey

Killed in action, 15 June 1917. Aged 23.
2nd Lieutenant, Machine Gun Company.
Arras Memorial, Pas de Calais, France. Bay 10.

Volunteering for service in September, 1914, he joined the University and Public Schools Battalion and was drafted to France in November 1915. There he saw several months' service in the trenches. In May, 1916, he returned to England to take up a commission, and a little later on he was sent to Grantham for a Machine Gun course.

In March of this year he returned to France and was in more than one battle previous to that of June 15th, when he made the last great sacrifice.

The OC the Company of the Royal Fusiliers to which Okey was attached during the actions said: – 'He displayed great courage and bravery, and carried on, after he had been wounded, until he met his death.'

L.A. Okey is the third of four brothers to fall in the war: the eldest is now out in France.

The school magazine, July 1917

There is no mention of this 'third brother', either in the school magazine or on the school War Memorial. Only Leslie and William Okey are listed.

William Ewart Okey

Killed in action in Mesopotamia, 21 January 1916. Aged 27.
2nd Lieutenant, 1st Connaught Rangers.
Amara War Cemetery, Iraq. IV. B. 20.

Captain H.T. Hewitt, 1st Connaught Rangers, in a letter to Mrs Okey, expresses the sympathy which 'all ranks of the regiment feel with you in your terrible loss. Your son was in my Company and was hit whilst gallantly leading his platoon against the Turkish position on January 21st. He was quite close to me when he was hit, first of all in the leg. One of his men tied up the wound and tried to get him under cover, but the place was absolutely devoid of cover, and he was subsequently hit in the side and died a few hours afterwards.'

The school magazine, March 1916

Wilfrid Omer-Cooper

Killed in action, 26 September 1916. Aged 21.
Private, Royal Fusiliers.
Thiépval Memorial, Somme, France. Pier and Face 12 D and 13 B.

On Friday, November 10th, his mother received official intimation that her son was killed in action on September 26th.

The school magazine, December 1916

The details of Wilfrid Cooper's death are not known. However, his obituary in the school magazine gives an impressive account of his distinguished scholarly work in zoological research. Young as he was, he was elected to the Linnean Society on the strength of several published works on Isopods, a group of crustaceans: 'Such an honour is given cautiously, and only to well-qualified persons, and rarely if ever has it been conferred upon one so young.'

Ronald Hodgson Daumier

Killed in action, 16 August 1917. Aged 21.
Private, 14th Battalion, London Scottish Regiment.
Perth Cemetery (China Wall), Ypres, West-Vlaanderen, Belgium. I. K. 47.

He was gazetted 2nd Lieutenant in the 5th Battalion of the Northumberland Fusiliers, but owing to a serious illness from which he suffered soon afterwards he was invalided out of the Army. An operation was performed on him, with success, and he gradually regained his health. Enlisting again (this time in the London Scottish), he was drafted to France, after a period of training at home, on June 8th, 1917. Little more than two months afterwards he made the great sacrifice, being killed in the action of August 16th.

The school magazine, December 1917

Roland Henry Peck

Killed in Mesopotamia, 12 March 1916. Aged 24.
2nd Lieutenant, Royal Flying Corps.
Basra Memorial, Iraq. Panel 22 and 63.

Peck was one of the first of our Old Boys to obtain a commission. He was gazetted to the 5th Dorsets, and after getting his second 'star' he was transferred to the Royal Flying Corps. He paid a visit to his old school just before leaving for France as an 'observer', where, as described in our last issue, he had at least one thrilling experience when scouting over the German lines.

The school magazine, March 1916

Roland Peck was subsequently sent to Mesopotamia and his name appears on the Basra Memorial in Iraq, which bears the names of more than 40,500 members of the Commonwealth forces who died in the operations in Mesopotamia from the autumn of 1914 to the end of August 1921, and whose graves are not known.

Jack Rodbard Phillips

Killed in action, 15 October 1917. Aged 25.
Gunner, Royal Garrison Artillery.
Divisional Collecting Post Cemetery, Ypres, West-Vlaanderen,
Belgium. B. 6.

With strong home ties, not to mention the importance of his work as a
cultivator of food, he might well have evaded military service. But the
call to arms was too strong for him, and, throwing up his career like so
many others of our gallant old boys, he joined the Army in July 1916.

Almost immediately afterwards he was sent to France, never to
return. Of the circumstances of his death nothing is yet known except
that he was killed by the bursting of a shell on October 15th 1917, and
that his body is buried in the Cemetery at St Jean, NE of Ypres.

The school magazine, March 1918

Arthur Lister Pickering

Killed on a minesweeper, 17 June 1917. Aged 17.
Signaller, RN.
Portsmouth Naval Memorial. 28.

The youngest* of our Old Boys to fall a victim to German lust of
power, Pickering occupies a prominent place in the memory of most
of the boys still at the school.

For twelve months before his death Pickering did the whole of the
signalling on HMT *Fraser*, which was sunk by a mine on June 17th.
Thirteen of the crew of seventeen were lost, and amongst those who
went down was poor Pickering.

The school magazine, July 1917

*In fact, William Alder was to be the youngest Old Boy to be killed,
dying just a month after Pickering, in July 1917. See pages 108–109.

Reginald Frank Purkess

Killed in action, February 23rd/24th, 1917. Aged 28.
Private, 1st/4th Battalion, Hampshire Regiment.
Basra Memorial, Iraq. Panel 21 and 63.

R.F. Purkess was one of the small band of 50 or so who joined the School when first it opened its doors sixteen years ago.

Wishing to enlist when the war broke out... he joined the Hampshire Regiment. In October, 1914, he went to India with his Battalion and completed his training there. He volunteered and was accepted for active service to Mesopotamia in October, 1916, taking part in the movements leading up to the glorious re-capture of Kut. His life, alas! was part of the price that had to be paid, for he fell there – killed in action – February 23rd–24th.

The school magazine, April 1917

Eric John Quaife

Killed in action, 30 June 1917. Aged 23.
Lieutenant, Royal Garrison Artillery.
Berks Cemetery Extension, Comines-Warneton, Hainaut, Belgium.
II. C. 21.

It appears that, in the early morning of June 30th, he, with another officer and some men, was occupying an Observation Post when it received a direct hit from a German shell, with the result that every member of the party was instantaneously killed.

The school magazine, July 1917

Eric Cecil Rey

Died of wounds, 11 October 1918. Aged 19.
Private, 10th Battalion, Royal West Kent Regiment.
Lijssenthoek Military Cemetery, Poperinge, West-Vlaanderen,
Belgium. XXX. B. 6.

The spirit that prompted E.C. Rey to volunteer for military service at
the age of 15 is, we are proud to think, typical of that which inspired so
many of our Old Boys to overcome every obstacle in the path leading
to self-sacrifice for their country's sake.

He joined the Cyclists' Corps of the 9th Hants in April, 1915, a few
weeks before attaining his 16th birthday. Soon after reaching the age
of 17 he was sent to France, attached to the 2nd Hants Infantry, and
took part in the fighting around Ypres in the late summer of 1916.
In the autumn he suffered from a form of poisoning and returned to
England with some hundreds of other boys, all under 18, collected
from various units. These were transferred to the Reserve Battalion
R.W. Kents and put into camp at Tunbridge Wells. There he remained
until Easter, 1918, when he returned to the Western Front and was
very soon engaged in fighting of the most severe kind.

On September 29, when in action near Ypres with Royal West
Kents, under General Plumer, he was severely wounded. Removed to
a casualty clearing station in the neighbourhood, he lingered for some
days, but finally passed away on October 11.

The school magazine, April 1919

Bernard Richardson

Killed in action, 22 October 1918. Aged 21.
Lance Corporal, 13th Kensington Battalion, London Regiment.
Heerstert Military Cemetery, Zwevegem, Belgium. C. 7.

He was killed in the attack on the ridge by Hoogmolen Mill on October 22, 1918. He was recommended for gallantry in the face of the enemy two months earlier (August 11), when, completely surrounded by hostile troops, he fought his way through to rejoin his Company.

The school magazine, March 1920

Sidney Hubert Seeviour, M./M.

Died of wounds, 28 August 1918. Aged 30.
Private, 2/4th Battalion, Hampshire Regiment.
Ligny-sur-Canche British Cemetery, Pas de Calais, France. A. 27.

While in India, in Egypt, and in Palestine with the 2/4th Hants he often enlivened the days of the battalion by reproductions of his beloved Gilbert and Sullivan Operas, as performed at school. Later on he was sent to France, and there he received his 'call.'

On the evening of the 27th of August he was admitted to a casualty clearing station, very seriously wounded in both legs and arms, and, after a few hours suffering, he expired in the early morning of the following day. The sad event gains additional pathos from the fact that he was engaged to be married, and that, before he received his wounds, a message was on the way to him granting him the leave of absence during which he was to have celebrated his wedding.

The school magazine, December 1918

Harold Spicer

Died, 6 May 1917. Aged 19.
Gunner, Royal Field Artillery.
Buried in St John's Churchyard, Moordown, Bournemouth.

He joined the 15th Reserve Battery, RFA, as Gunner on January 15th, 1917, and was about to proceed to France on April 28th when he was taken ill with erysipelas and meningitis. He was removed to Hospital at Salisbury, where everything possible was done to save him, but without avail. He died on May 6th and brought home for burial in St John's Churchyard, Moordown.

The school magazine, July 1917

Francis Noel Tallant

Drowned at sea off the south coast of Ireland, 4 October 1918. Aged 22.
Eastern Telegraph Company.

(Employed by the Eastern Telegraph Company...)... he was transferred to Malta, and then to Aden, from which latter place he arrived home on furlough last April.

Having accepted service for a further period of five years, Tallant was selected for duty at Cape Town, a station much appreciated in the service, and, embarking at Birkenhead with two colleagues at the end of September on the Japanese liner *Hirano Maru*, he met his untimely fate when this steamer was torpedoed off the South Coast of Ireland on October 4th.

Though not in 'khaki', Tallant is as fully entitled to a place on our Roll of Honour as if he had fallen in battle, for his occupation was regarded as of such vital importance in the prosecution of the war, that he, with other cable operators was debarred by the Government from taking service with the Colours.

The school magazine, December 1918

The *Hirano Maru* was torpedoed by an enemy submarine, 60 miles off the south coast of Ireland and sank in 7 minutes. Only eleven passengers were saved.

Sydney Henry Thrift

Missing, believed killed, 14 July 1916. Aged 26.
2nd Lieutenant, Cheshire Regiment.
Thiépval Memorial, Pier and Face 3 C and 4 A.

Soon after the war broke out he was offered a commission and was gazetted to the Cheshire Regiment.

The last news of him was contained in a letter dated 13th July, 1916, in which he stated that he had not had his boots off for thirteen days. A thrilling account of the part he played in the great advance is given in the following passage: – 'I am writing this in a Hun trench which we took last night: we crawled up in the dark about 600 yards, and then rushed him and seized three of his strong points. We only lost two or three men. We bombed him out and he ran like fury, shouting. We have since bombed him further and further away and are blocking up his way back. He is kicking up a row and counter-bombing, but Company is dealing with him now. We have been troubled by his snipers a bit.'

2nd-Lieut. Thrift was married in May, 1915... He leaves a widow and a little son, 14 months old, to mourn his loss.

The school magazine, July 1917

Horace Murray Tollemache

Killed in action, 17 July 1918. Aged 27.
Lieutenant, 15th Battalion, Hampshire Regiment.
Lijssenthoek Military Cemetery, Poperinge, West-Vlaanderen, Belgium. XXVIII D. 11.

H.M. Tollemache, son of the late Hon. Murray Arthur Tollemache and the Hon. Mrs. Murray Tollemache, was one of seven brothers, all of whom have fought in the war.

The outbreak of the war found him in Canada, when he at once threw up his employment to enlist. He came over with the First Canadian Contingent, proceeded immediately to France, and was wounded at the Second Battle of Ypres, in April 1915. He obtained his commission in the Hampshire Regiment in July 1915, and was again wounded during the Battle of the Somme in September 1916. In that action he distinguished himself and was mentioned in dispatches 'for his gallantry during the attack on Flers in leading and inspiring his men, though wounded, and remaining in the captured trench for 14 hours.' He had been overseas five times previous to being killed in action.

The school magazine, December 1918

John Reginald Turner

Killed in action, 13 October 1914. Aged 21.
Lieutenant, 3rd Battalion, Dorset Regiment.
Guards Cemetery, Windy Corner, Cuinchy, Pas de Calais. III. T. 21.

Turner joined the Special Reserve of Officers soon after leaving school, and was one of the first to be called upon for service in France.

He came safely through the retreat from Mons, but fell on October 13th, when conducting a retirement of his platoon under very heavy fire from artillery and infantry.

The school magazine, December 1914

Ranulph Kingsley Joyce Vallings

Killed in action, 13 January 1917. Aged 23.
Flight Sub-Lieutenant, RN.
Mikra British Cemetery, Kalamaria, Greece. 1870.

In August, 1914, he enlisted in the London Cyclists' Battalion. He obtained a commission in the RNVR in December, 1915, and in due course he qualified as a pilot and was transferred to the RN.

The school magazine, April 1917

The precise details of how and where Vallings was killed are not recorded in the school magazine.

Sydney Douglas Watkins

Died of pneumonia, 13 April 1915. Aged 23.
Appointed Temporary Sub-Lieutenant RNR.
The details of where Watkins died and was buried are not recorded.

After leaving school, Watkins took service with the Royal Mail Steam Packet Company, and in August 1914, he was appointed Second Officer of the RMSP *Teviot*.

After the outbreak of the war he was engaged in transport duty, when he unfortunately caught a chill, which ultimately proved fatal.

The school magazine, July 1915

William Kingsbury Webber

Killed in action, 22 August 1918. Aged 27.
Lance Corporal, Artists' Rifles.
Vis-en-Artois Memorial, Pas de Calais, France, Panel 10.

He joined the Artists' Rifles OTC in November, 1914. He proceeded to France the following February and was with his Battalion there and in Flanders for 3½ years, returning to England only for occasional brief furloughs. The last of these was in the early spring of this year, just before the great German onslaught on Peronne. Webber came through this retreat, only to fall just as the tide of success was turning in favour of the allied cause. Webber had been deputed, on August 20th, to bring water and rations to his Battalion. The operation involved a two-days' march across ground which was under heavy shell-fire from the Germans, and Webber had almost succeeded in taking his party to their objective, when, in Logeast Wood, near Achiet, an enemy shell struck and felled a tree immediately above him. Poor Webber was killed instantly.

The school magazine, December 1918

Frederick John White

Killed in action, 8 June 1918. Aged 25.
Private, A Company, 1st Platoon, 6th Dorset Regiment.
Pozières Memorial, Somme, France. Panel 48.

He 'joined up' in March 1916. Trained at first with the Somerset Light Infantry, his health broke down, and he was transferred to several different units before being sent to the 6th Dorsets. He was drafted to France in May, 1917, but fell out in August, and was sent to a base hospital to recuperate. There he was very ill, but, on his discharge, he was again sent up the line and was in active service till March, 1918, when he returned on a 'leave' which – poor fellow – he had to spend mostly in a Military Hospital.

On May 2, he returned, still unfit, to France. Five weeks later, the end came when, in a night attack at Mailly, Thiépval Ridge, on June 8, he and so many other men of the Dorsets went over the top never to return.

The school magazine, December 1919

John Clifford Williams

Died, 16 April 1917. Aged 28.
Sergeant, 9th Field Ambulance, RAMC.
St. Sever Cemetery Extension, Rouen, Seine-Maritime, France. O. IX. D. 1.

... he emigrated along with his people to British Columbia. The call to arms, however, found in him a ready response: he returned to help his motherland, and, early in 1916, we hear of him on active service in France. There he remained, serving his country, until he was carried off, a victim to kidney disease, last April.

The school magazine, March 1918

John Hubert Winton

Killed in action, 7 July 1916. Aged 18.
2nd Lieutenant, 9th Battalion, Northumberland Fusiliers.
Ovillers Military Cemetery, Somme, France. VII. C. 1.

Winton joined the Northumberland Fusiliers as soon as he was old enough. He quickly rose to the rank of sergeant, and went to France in September, 1915, as bomber sergeant. After going through the Battle of Loos he was engaged in the trenches until March, 1916.

Later on... he was gazetted 2nd Lieutenant in the 9th Battalion, Northumberland Fusiliers. [See opposite for letter by his Commanding Officer].

Arthur Wolfe

Killed in action, 11 March 1915. Aged 22.
Private, 4th Battalion, Seaforth Highlanders.
Le Touret Memorial, Pas de Calais, France. Panel 38 and 39.

INFORMING GRIEVING PARENTS

Here is another typical letter sent home, describing the way in which 2nd Lieutenant Winton met his death. His Commanding Officer, Lieutenant Colonel Bryan, wrote:

Mine is the sad task of writing to the relatives of those we lost in action on the 7th inst., when your son, 2nd-Lieut. J.H. Winton who was leading his men to the assault when last seen, is believed to have been killed. In the confusion and turmoil of an attack by night, it is very difficult to tell the exact time when an officer was last seen alive, and I should be raising false hopes, I fear, if I held out the expectation that your son may yet be alive. I pray that he may be, but you must be prepared for the confirmation of his death.

School Magazine, July 1916

On the outbreak of war he enlisted in the 4th Battalion, Seaforth Highlanders, and early in January his unit was called into service at the front. His two letters, published on another page (the school magazine, March 1915) give a vivid account of his experiences. A week after he had written the last of these came the great attack at Neuve Chapelle, in which poor Wolfe was killed.

Reginald Gilbert Wrenn

Killed in action, 29 June 1918. Aged 23.
Private, Canadian Expeditionary Force.
Longuenesse (St Omer) Souvenir Cemetery, Pas de Calais, France.
V. C. 20.

On leaving school he went to Canada, and it was there, at Edmonton, Alberta, in August, 1914, that he enlisted in the Canadian Expeditionary Force, and in due course went with the Division to France. He fought uninjured in the second battle of Ypres, when the Germans made their first gas attack, and similar good fortune attended him in the subsequent battles of St Julien, Festubert, and Givenchy. His Sergt.-Major mentioned him for brave deeds several times.

On one occasion he volunteered, with seven others, for an important and dangerous duty. Six of these men were killed and one wounded, and Private Wrenn was the only one to survive.

He was eventually transferred to the unit of his brother Frank, who also came over with the Canadian Forces, and who records in a letter to his parents that his brother was killed by a bomb dropped by an enemy aeroplane right on the hut in which he was sleeping.

His brother Frank speaks of him as follows: – 'Every man of the unit speaks of Reg. as the bravest man they have ever met. On many occasions in the past he demonstrated acts of bravery. We buried him at 2 p.m. on Sunday afternoon, June 30th, and the whole unit attended the funeral.'

The school magazine, December 1918

Frederick Royston Young

Accidentally killed, 31 August 1918. Aged 19.
2nd Lieutenant, RAF
Beverley (St Mary) Church Cemetery, Yorkshire. T. 31.

... he was recommended for a commission in the RAF (then RFC), and two months later he proceeded to Hastings – as a cadet – for a ten weeks' course. This was followed by a six weeks' course at the School of Aeronautics, Oxford, at the conclusion of which he was gazetted 2nd Lieutenant on February 21st.

Later, after a six weeks' 'leave', he was posted in succession to Flying Schools at Doncaster, and Beverley. It was at the latter place that he met with the accident which cost him his life. He had already made several 'solo' flights, and, at 7.30 in the morning of August 31st, attempted for the first time to fly a 'camel' or single-seated service machine of the latest type, when, for some unexplained reason, control was lost at a height of 80 to 100 feet. The machine crashed to earth, and poor Young received such severe injuries that he succumbed about four hours later.

The school magazine, December 1918

THE ARMISTICE
– SOME THOUGHTS OF THE SURVIVORS

From A.H. Rogers, in France (a member of staff at Bournemouth School)

At last! I hope and trust now that there will be no objection to my being with you once more for next term. I feel very thankful that the war has come to an end while I am out here, for I cannot conceive that hostilities will be renewed.

I don't expect anyone in England can conceive the feelings of the people out here when the news came through. Very lights and rockets were sent up all over the place and I should think every flashlight in our lines was turned on. I don't think any of us quite realises the situation; it has literally taken our breath away.

I am devoutly thankful that I have a whole skin at the present moment.

The school magazine, December 1918

GRIEF AND PRIDE: A SISTER WRITES
A LETTER THAT SPEAKS FOR ALL

Dear Dr Fenwick,

My father and I appreciate very deeply all the kindly and heartfelt sympathy you have given us on the occasion of the death in action of my brother Frank. We thank you most sincerely. It is a bitter sorrow, but there is with it, as you say, the pride of knowing that he gave himself in the great cause – and that thought brings courage.

Frank lost his life while leading his platoon in an attack over open ground on the morning of July 14th [1916] in the face of very heavy fire from machine-guns and rifles. It was his first time in action, having been in the trenches but a day and a night since joining the regiment on July 1st.

We are most grateful for the deep sympathy of the masters and boys with whom it was his pleasure to work, and shall always have an affectionate interest in the school to which he has endeared himself.

With our good wishes and kindest regards,

Yours sincerely,

Mary F -------

From the date given in the letter above, it is likely that Frank lost his life in the Battle of the Somme.

From Lieutenant N. Wragg, in France

It looks as if the war is over at last, though we mustn't make too certain. I can't tell you how glad I am to have been in at the death. I think it will be always one of the 'prides' of my life.

We were busy chasing after the Boche (for one could hardly call it pushing him back; we had been unable to find him!) on the Monday morning of the 11th, when at 8 a.m. the news came through, 'Advance cancelled; hostilities cease 11 a.m.', on which I think we went wild for an hour or so.

The school magazine, December 1918

From Lieutenant J. S. Hughes, RAF

Well, it's all over now, and, like nearly every other young fellow in like case, I feel rather stunned to find that I've come out with two arms and legs and more or less sane.

The school magazine, December 1918

THE FINAL RECKONING

Served:	622 Old Boys	24 Masters	5 Caretakers
Killed:	98 – 94 Old Boys and 4 Masters		
Wounded:	95 – many with two, three, four, or even more wounds		
MC awards:	18 (A.H. Baker winning an MC and Bar)		

Appendix 1

DATES, FACTS AND FIGURES

DEATHS, MONTH BY MONTH

1914

Date	Name	Killed in action unless otherwise specified	Country of Death	Age
17 Sept	Tiplady H. (master)	Died of appendicitis	England	26
13 Oct	Turner J.R.		France	21
7 Nov	Atkin J.M. (master)		Belgium	23

1915

19 Feb	Moorey F.L.	Died of septic poisoning	France	20
11 Mar	Wolfe A.J.		France	22
13 Apr	Watkins S.D.	Died of pneumonia	Unknown	23
25 May	Hazard D.G.		France	21
5 July	Heather C.A.		Turkey	20
10 Aug	Mills A.G.		Turkey	17
6 Sept	Durham H. L.		Dardanelles	21
10 Oct	Budden H.R.		France	20

| 2 Nov | Hickling E.R.E. | Shot by a prisoner (*see page 137–138*) | France | 19 |

1916

5 Jan	Goldsmith O.	Died of septic poisoning	England	17
16 Jan	Ingram G.E.		France	24
21 Jan	Okey W.E.		Mesopotamia	27
12 Mar	Peck R.H.		Mesopotamia	24
6 April	Cooper C.H.		France	18
29 May	Cornwell J.		France	24
31 May	Meyer H.W.	Drowned	Sinking of HMS *Queen Mary*	20
5 June	Barrow N.	Drowned	Sinking of HMS *Hampshire*	22
5 June	Butler R.T.	Drowned	Sinking of HMS *Hampshire*	20
5 June	Lonsdale T.W. MC		France	22
26 June	Pean P.D.F. (master)		France	29
7 July	Goodall C.C.		France	25
7 July	Winton J.H.		France	18
13 July	Challis W.G.F.		France	24
13 July	Kent L.J.		France	19
14 July	Baker W.P.		France	28
14 July	Forman F. (master)		France	28
14 July	Thrift S.H.		France	26
9 Aug	Farwell H.G.H.		France	27
15 Sept	Bailey W.G.W.		France	20

16 Sept	Hollies H.J.		France	26
26 Sept	Cooper W.O.		France	21
26 Sept	Harbord C.E.		France	20
31 Oct	Gunning W.H.	Died of wounds	Malta	23
13 Nov	Graham C.	Died of malaria	Egypt	23
22 Nov	Horsey C.J.	Died of wounds	France	25
26 Nov	Finch H.W.	Died of wounds	France	21

1917

12 Jan	Kelly F.W.		Mesopotamia	23
13 Jan	Vallings R.K.J.		Greece	23
23 Feb	Purkess R.F.		Mesopotamia	28
4 Mar	Hands L.H.	Died of wounds	France	21
26 Mar	Hodges F.O.		Gaza	31
16 Apr	Williams J.C.	Died of kidney disease	France	28
6 May	Spicer H.	Died of erysipelas and meningitis	England	19
15 June	Okey L.A.		France	23
17 June	Pickering A.L.	Drowned	Sinking of HMT *Fraser*	17
30 June	Quaife E.J.		France	23
27 July	Froud H.W.		France	28
30 July	Alder W.A.R		France	17
31 July	Budden R.A.		France	19
16 Aug	New B.B.		France	26
16 Aug	Paumier R.H.		France	21
7 Sept	Dawson J.M.	Accidentally killed (RAF)	England	20
11 Sept	Kent F.E.		France	19

4 Oct	Martin C.S.		France	26
15 Oct	Phillips J.R.		France	25
16 Oct	Butler A.S.		France	24
26 Oct	Moorey W.E.	Died of wounds	France	26
30 Oct	Colborne R.		France	25
20 Nov	May J.H.		France	21
2 Dec	Bailey W.J.		France	29

1918

21 Mar	Martyn H.H.		France	20
25 Mar	Ayling E.P.A.		France	25
28 Mar	Collingwood G.F.		France	25
9 Apr	Floyd H.G.		Palestine	20
14 May	Cheshire R.W.	Died of wounds	France	19
21 May	Hame A.W.		France	26
7 June	Game F.E.	Died from poison gas	France	21
29 June	Wrenn R.G.		France	23
8 June	White F.J.		France	25
17 July	Tollemache H.M.		Belgium	27
21 July	Hunt G.E.	Accidentally killed (RAF)	England	20
29 July	Bell L.	Accidentally killed (RAF)	England	19
8 Aug	Croft H.G.		France	18
22 Aug	Webber W.K.		France	27
28 Aug	Seeviour S.H.	Died of wounds	France	30
31 Aug	Nutman J.D.		France	19
31 Aug	Young F.	Accidentally killed (RAF)	England	19

12 Sept	Cooper O.I.		France	20
17 Sept	Deans H.M.		France	24
18 Sept	Barnes B.F.		France	22
19 Sept	Dyason R.C.	Died from poison gas	France	20
24 Sept	Marshall E.G.		France	25
4 Oct	Johnson P.J.	Drowned	Drowned at sea	27
4 Oct	Tallant F.N.	Drowned	Drowned at sea	22
8 Oct	Jones A.N.C.	Died of pneumonia	England	18
11 Oct	Rey E.C.	Died of wounds	France	19
14 Oct	Bishop A.W.		France	20
18 Oct	Hazel W.R.	Died of malaria	Egypt	21
22 Oct	Richardson B.		Belgium	21
27 Oct	Hill E.A.	Died of wounds	France	23
14 Nov	Jefferis F.S.	Died of pneumonia	England	18
23 Nov	Mosley A.R.		France	22

1919

3 Feb	Allbon B.C.J.	Died in hospital	Wounded in France	22
20 Dec	Cuthbert L.A.		India	21

1920

Feb 21	Holland H.L.	Drowned at sea (RAF)	Irish Sea	21

THE NINETY-EIGHT WHO WERE KILLED

Service & arm in which they served

ROYAL NAVY	4
ROYAL NAVAL DIVISION	1

ROYAL NAVY AIR SERVICE	2
ARMY CAVALRY	2
ARTILLERY	9
ENGINEERS	2
INFANTRY	64
ROYAL RMY MEDICAL CORPS	1
ROYAL FLYING CORPS / RAF	7
MERCHANT NAVY	1
CIVILIANS	3
AUSTRALIAN INFANTRY	1
CANADIAN ARMY SERVICE CORPS	1

DEATHS YEAR BY YEAR (1914–1920)

1914:   5
1915:   8
1916:   26
1917:   25
1918:   31
1919:   2
1920:   1

THE FIRST AND LAST TO DIE BETWEEN
4 AUGUST 1914 & 11 NOVEMBER 1918
The first
13 October 1914. Aged 21.
Lieutenant J. R. Turner, 3rd Battalion, the Dorsetshire Regiment.
Buried in the Guards Cemetery, Windy Corner, Cuinchy, Pas de Calais,
France. Grave III. T. 21.

The last

26 October 1918. Aged 23.

Major E. A. Hill, 8th Battalion, Royal Sussex Regiment.

Buried in the Villers-Bretonneux Military Cemetery, Somme, France.

Grave XVIA. B.20.

THE FOUR YOUNGEST TO DIE
– ALL AGED SEVENTEEN

The youngest

Pioneer William Arthur Redvers Alder. Aged 17 years and 67 days.

55th Division, Signal Coy. Royal Engineers.

Died 31 July 1917.

Buried in the Potijze Chateau Lawn Cemetery, Ypres, Belgium.

The Commonwealth War Graves Commission record shows his age as 20, but school records show he was born 24 May 1900. He probably lied about his age.

The second youngest

Boy Arthur Lister Pickering. Aged 17 years and 198 days.

HM Trawler *Fraser*.

Died 17 June 1917.

Commemorated on the Portsmouth Naval Memorial, Hampshire.

The third youngest

Private Oliver Goldsmith. Aged 17 years and 240 days.

Hampshire Yeomanry (Carabiniers).

Died 5 January 1916.

Buried in the Wimborne Road Cemetery, Bournemouth. Grave I.3.18.N.

The fourth youngest

Private Alfred George Mills. Aged 17 years and 342 days.

10th Battalion, The Hampshire Regiment.

Died 10 August 1915.
Commemorated on the Helles Memorial, Turkey.

The eldest to die
Private Sydney Hubert Seeviour, M.M. Aged 30.
2/4th Battalion, The Hampshire Regiment.
Died 28 August 1918.
Buried in the Ligny-Sur-Canche British Cemetery, Pas de Calais.
Grave A.27.

Private Seeviour was awarded the Military Medal for bringing in wounded Australians the day before he was killed.

COUNTRIES WHERE OLD BOYS FROM BOURNEMOUTH SCHOOL ARE BURIED OR COMMEMORATED

Country	Buried in Cemeteries	Commemorated on Memorials
Belgium	15	4
Egypt	1	–
France	30	15
Greece	2	–
India	1	–
Iraq	2	2
Malta	1	–
Syria	1	–
Turkey	2	1
United Kingdom	13	6 (includes those who died at sea)

Appendix 2

DECORATIONS GAINED

MASTERS AND OLD BOYS WHO GAINED MILITARY DECORATIONS

MASTERS

Day J.P.	Mentioned in Dispatches
Williams, Rev. W.J.	Military Cross

OLD BOYS

Austin W.B.	Military Cross
Baker A.H.	Military Cross and Bar
Copp A.F.	Military Cross
Cuthbert L.A. ★★	Military Cross
Dinwoodie H.	Military Cross
Drayton R.	Military Cross
Gunning E.F.	Mentioned in Dispatches
Hame B.W.	Military Cross and Mentioned in Dispatches
Head H.G.	Military Cross
Henry J.L.	Mentioned in Dispatches
Hill E.A. ★★	Military Cross
Hillier H.	Distinguished Flying Cross

Holland E.	Belgian Croix de Guerre and Mentioned in Dispatches
Howard A.C.	Military Cross
Jones J.G.C.	Military Cross and Mentioned in Dispatches
Lonsdale T.W. ★★	Military Cross and Mentioned in Dispatches
Maddox E.R.	Military Cross
Martin L.J.	Military Cross
Mead R.	Mentioned in Dispatches
Moriarty J.	Military Cross
Mossop F.J.	Belgian Croix de Guerre
Mossop G.P.	Mentioned in Dispatches
Osborne F.W.	Mentioned in Dispatches
Peck R.H. ★★	Mentioned in Dispatches
Phillips H.T.	Mentioned in Dispatches
Preiss E.C.	Military Medal
Seeviour S.H. ★★	Military Medal
Short H.A.	Military Cross
Sims C.J.	Distinguished Flying Cross
Snelgar E.E.	Distinguished Conduct Medal
Snelgar J.T.	Member of the British Empire
Tollemache A.H.	Mentioned in Dispatches
Tollemache H.M. ★★	Mentioned in Dispatches
Turner G.A.	Mentioned in Dispatches
Whiting A.	Military Cross
Wragg N.	Military Cross

★★ Killed in action

THE MILITARY CROSS & THE MILITARY MEDAL

The Military Cross was instituted on 28 December 1914, as a means of formally recognising the courage of junior officers of the rank of Captain or below and also for Warrant Officers – officially awarded 'for gallantry in the field'.

It complemented the Military Medal, which was awarded to servicemen below officer rank, and was instituted on 25 March 1916, and back-dated to 1914.

Awards of the Military Cross were announced in the *London Gazette* with a citation. Altogether, 37,081 MCs were awarded during the First World War, plus 2,992 first Bars, 176 second Bars, and 4 third Bars.

In 1931 the award of the Military Cross was extended to Majors and also to members of the Royal Air Force for actions on the ground.

Since the review of the honours system in 1993, which was designed to remove distinctions of rank in awards for bravery, the Military Medal, formerly the third-level decoration for other ranks, has been discontinued. The Military Cross now serves as the third-level award for gallantry on land for all ranks of the British Armed Forces.

EPILOGUE – 1919

In common with towns, villages and communities throughout the world, Bournemouth School felt it necessary to have a War Memorial listing the names of those who fell during the Great War. In the school magazine of July 1919, Dr Fenwick appealed for contributions to make a worthy permanent memorial. His final comments on the war make a fitting epilogue to this book. He entitled it 'Peace'.

PEACE

The cessation of hostilities brought about by the Armistice of November 11, 1918, has been ratified by the Treaty of Peace signed at Versailles on June 28, 1919. So ends the most colossal war in history.

This is not the place for a review of the tragedy which has darkened our lives for nearly five years, nor has the time yet come when the various events which led up to the triumphant conclusion can be viewed in their correct perspective.

We stand, indeed too close to the conflagration of the past few years to be able to award praise in just proportion in each of the many factors which saved us, and, with us, all who value truth, freedom, justice, and liberty, from a fate to which death itself would seem infinitely preferable.

About the vastness of the debt, however, which we owe to our fighting men we can be under no delusion, for to them most of all must gratitude be shown for the blessings of peace, unless, indeed, we are to be found unworthy of the great heritage which by their heroism they have bequeathed to us.

Amongst these fighting men we point with legitimate pride to that gallant band which left the school to fight for King and Country. Their great self-sacrifice we feel it our particular privilege and duty so to recognise that some imperishable memorial, raised by past and present members and friends of the school, may bear constant testimony to the gratitude we feel so deeply.

As it is only by a memorial such as this that these priceless memories can be kept green, those who love the school and cherish its fair name will no doubt see to it that, in future years, it shall not be said of her that she knew not how to honour her bravest sons.

Dr Fenwick, writing in the school magazine, July 1919

EPILOGUE –
TWENTY-FIRST CENTURY

A century has passed since Dr Fenwick was teaching the generation of boys whose war experiences make up this book. Arguably, we are now in a better position to view that war – as Fenwick put it – in a 'correct perspective'. Sadly, we can now realise that this was not a 'war to end all wars' – nor did the survivors return to a plentiful supply of 'homes for heroes'.

Since then, the world has witnessed the collapse of the well-intentioned League of Nations and has suffered a Second World War, immediately followed by the Cold War, and then by an appalling series of further deadly conflicts.

It would be easy to be cynical and view humanity with despair.

However, in compiling these personal records of a representative group of participants of the First World War, I have felt an overwhelming sense of admiration and pride in the sheer exuberance and vitality expressed throughout their writings.

These young men were not 'heroes'; not in the accepted romantic sense of the word – but they were bursting with energy and determination to do the horrible tasks which they knew had to be done, and to enjoy whatever they could of the comradeship resulting from their proximity to death. They wrote home to Dr Fenwick, their father-figure of a headmaster, with cheerfulness and good humour, hoping for – and indeed receiving – his constant sympathy and approval.

Having completed this anthology, and having followed these vibrant young men in their extraordinary wartime roles, I am filled with humble gratitude to them all.

My comfortable life would not have been possible without their sacrifice.

At the going down of the sun, and in the morning
We will remember them...

David Hilliam, former deputy headmaster of Bournemouth School

FURTHER READING

Brophy, John & Partridge, Eric, *Dictionary of Tommies' Songs and Slang* (Frontline Books, 2008)

Brown, Malcolm, *The Imperial War Museum Book of the Somme* (Sidgwick & Jackson, 1996)

Brown, Malcolm, *Tommy Goes to War* (Tempus, 2001)

Campbell, Christy, *Band of Brigands: The First Men in Tanks* (Harper Press, 2007)

Cross, Robin, *In Memoriam – Remembering The Great War* (Ebury Press, 2008)

Fowler, Simon, *Tracing your First World War Ancestors* (Countryside Books, 2003)

Messenger, Charles, *World War I in Colour* (Ebury Press, London, 2003)

Midddlebrook, Martin, *The First Day on the Somme* (Penguin Books, 1984)

Prior, Robin and Wilson, Trevor, *The First World War* (Cassell, 1999)

Strachan, Hew, *The First World War* (Simon & Schuster, UK Ltd, 2003)

Sutherland, Jon & Canwell, Diane, *The Battle of Jutland* (Pen & Sword Books, 2007)

Treadwell, Terry & Wood, Alan C., *The First Air War* (Brassey's Ltd, 1996)

WEBSITES

www.1914-1918.net (About the British Army in the First World War)

www.bbc.co.uk/history/war/wwone/index.html (The BBC's guide to the First World War)

www.firstworldwar.com (Many aspects of the war, also battlefield tourism)

www.regiments.org (History of units of the British Army)

www.battlefields1418.50megs.com (Visiting battlefields)

INDEX